BONAVENTURE

A Play in Three Acts

by

CHARLOTTE HASTINGS

SAMUEL   FRENCH

LONDON

NEW YORK   TORONTO   SYDNEY   HOLLYWOOD

BONAVENTURE

Produced at the Vaudeville Theatre, London, on December 6th, 1949, with the following cast of characters :

(in the order of their appearance)

NURSE PHILLIPS	*Betty England*
NURSE BRENT	*Josephine Douglas*
SISTER JOSEPHINE	*Nell Ballantyne*
WILLY PENTRIDGE	*John Crocker*
SISTER MARY BONAVENTURE	*Fay Compton*
DR JEFFREYS	*Ballard Berkeley*
THE MOTHER SUPERIOR	*Deirdre Doyle*
MELLING	*Colin Douglas*
SARAT CARN	*Mary Kerridge*
MISS PIERCE	*Mary Marvin*
MARTHA PENTRIDGE	*Cicely Walper*

The Play directed by Charles Hickman.

SYNOPSIS OF SCENES

The action of the play passes in the Convent of Our Lady of Rheims, a French Nursing Order, at Denzil St David, a village some miles from Norwich, England. The time is the beginning of 1947.

ACT I
The Great Hall of the Convent. About 6 p.m.

ACT II
SCENE 1.—Sister Mary's room. Two hours later.
SCENE 2.—The same. Next evening.

ACT III
SCENE 1.—The same. Next afternoon.
SCENE 2.—The Great Hall. Three hours later.

(Should it be found too difficult to make the scene change in Act III, it is suggested that Act III, Scene 1, be played as a third scene to Act II).

BONAVENTURE*

ACT I

SCENE.—*The Great Hall of the Convent of Our Lady of Rheims, a French Nursing Order, at Denzil St David, a village some miles from Norwich, England. About 6 p.m. on an evening at the beginning of 1947.*

The Great Hall is a magnificent room ; the walls are built of plain grey stone blocks, the roof is vaulted and supported on three pillars, one each R. and L., and one up C. Recessed R.C. of the back wall is a great Gothic window, reaching nearly to the ceiling and filled with fine stained glass, depicting the Visitation of the Angel to the Virgin. Under this window is a great oak door which opens inwards. When the door is open a low wall can be seen, with a view behind it of flood waters stretching away into the distance. Back stage, L. of the window, an oak staircase mounts to a small gallery from which two more steps lead to a door L. At the top of the stairs, facing the audience, is a door that leads to the Hospital. A notice, " To Hospital. Staff only " is neatly painted on a board affixed to the wall L. of the door. Down L. is a wide stone-hooded fireplace in which a cheerful log fire burns in a metal fire-basket. Above the fireplace is a door that leads to the Mother Superior's room. Down R. an arched opening leads to the main part of the Convent. A big carved sideboard with two drawers, stands above the arch down R. On it is a brightly polished brass bowl, and a modern internal telephone. Against the wall up R., above the pillar, there is a long oak chest. A statue of the Virgin and Child stands on a pedestal lit by a small red lamp. The hearth is furnished with large firedogs and has a rush mat in front of it. An ebony crucifix hangs on the canopy above the fireplace. Coffin-stools stand R. and L. of the fireplace, and there is another stool down R. A carved armchair with a high back is placed R. of the fireplace, in such a position that anyone sitting in it is not visible from the stairs. R.C. at a slight angle is a long refectory table, with plain rush-seated chairs above it, and at each end of it. A low bench stands below it. The hall is lit by wall electric candle brackets, one C. of the wall R. and the other below the fireplace. There are also two electric lights in iron lantern fittings, one over the staircase and the other in the arch down R. The light switches are above the fireplace.

(See the Ground Plan and Photograph of the Scene.)

---

*N.B. Paragraph 3 on page ii of this Acting Edition regarding photo-copying and video-recording should be carefully read.

For a few moments before the CURTAIN *rises, the Convent bell is heard.*

When the CURTAIN *rises, the bell fades out. It is about six o'clock in the evening, and in the dim light the great room has a calm and sombre beauty. The electric lights have not been switched on, and the last of the fading daylight shines through the stained-glass window. The rain and wind are beating and howling outside. The table is set for two, one place above it, and one at the* R. *end.* NURSE PHILLIPS, *a grave-looking girl, is seated in the chair above the table. She wears a trim mauve and white striped uniform, white apron and a small white cap set well back on her head. She has finished her meal and is reading a newspaper. She glances up at the windows as the rain increases, then returns to her paper. As she does so,* NURSE BRENT *enters excitedly by the Hospital door and clatters down the stairs to* L. *of the table. She is younger than* NURSE PHILLIPS. *She wears a similar uniform, but her flowing cap is pinned insecurely over untidy curls. She has a dark damp shoulder cape on over her uniform.*

BRENT (*as she enters*). Flippers, Flippers— (*she pulls off her cape*) they're getting out boats and sandbags in the village. They say the Great Dyke may come down.

PHILLIPS (*without looking up*). No doubt your hair is down in sympathy already. And *stop* calling me Flippers.

BRENT (*turning and moving to the fireplace*). Oh, don't be so superior. (*She spreads her damp cape over the stool below the fireplace, then stands with her back to the fire, warming her hands behind her and talking without a pause*). Just hark at that wind. They say the waters haven't been so high for a hundred years.

PHILLIPS. And who precisely are *they ?*

BRENT. I wish you wouldn't talk in capital letters. People in the village, of course. And Sister Josephine and Sister Agnes— and Willy.

PHILLIPS (*contemptuously*). Willy !

BRENT. He knows more about the weather, and cattle and trees— and things—than most normal people. (*She moves eagerly to the chair* L. *of the table and kneels on it.*) I wonder what Josie's making for supper—I'm starving. What did you have ?

(PHILLIPS *impatiently puts down the paper and looks at the small fob watch that is pinned to her uniform.*)

PHILLIPS. Brent, for heaven's sake stop talking. You're on duty in—nineteen and three-quarter minutes precisely. And *do* something about your hair. If Sister Mary sees you . . .

BRENT. She won't be stuffy. She's got a sense of humour. (*She picks up a book from the table and turns the pages, still babbling cheerfully.*) Until I came here I thought all nuns were very calm and detached. I didn't expect them to laugh and be approachable like other people. I suppose it's because this is a nursing Order. They're not out of touch with the world.

PHILLIPS. There's not sufficient *discipline* here. Sometimes I'm really surprised at Sister Mary's attitude to the patients. A qualified woman with her authority—after all, she *is* Matron.

BRENT. You know what she says. " Don't nag them. They'll get well quicker if they're happy." (*She replaces the book on the table, rises, takes several peanuts from her pocket, cracks them and eats them.*

PHILLIPS. A hospital can't be run entirely on kindness. Now when I was at the Memorial Hospital in . . .

BRENT (*moving to the fireplace*). I know—you've told us. Everyone went around in iron corsets, and when the house surgeon appeared no-one was allowed to breathe until he was out of sight. (*She cracks another nut.*) Catch me holding my breath for Dr Jeffreys, I must say.

PHILLIPS. Don't be disrespectful to the medical staff. And *stop* chewing those disgusting nuts.

BRENT. All right—all right. (*She throws the nut-shells into the fire.*) Bless us, at this rate you'll be mummified before you're thirty.

PHILLIPS. The prospect need not affect you. I'm leaving at the end of this month.

BRENT (*moving to L. of the table*). But how silly—this is a grand place to train. Mary's a wonderful teacher—and the food's superb.

PHILLIPS. I don't like the lax atmosphere. And I object to that horrible Willy prowling about. (*She picks up the newspaper and starts to read.*)

BRENT. Willy's all right if you don't show your aversion. The poor thing couldn't help being born. D'you know your real trouble —you've no patience.

(SISTER JOSEPHINE *enters briskly down* R. *She is a short buxom Scotswoman, rosy and wrinkled, with bright twinkling eyes and a deep rich voice. She wears the habit of the French religieuse, a fitted tunic and full-gathered skirt of rich blue, a black apron, square white starched collar, and a wide white cornette—the mediaeval winged head-dress—and a leather girdle with a trailing wooden rosary attached to it. She carries a tray with* BRENT'S *supper on it.*)

JOSEPHINE (*as she enters*). And you, young lady, have no hairpins. (*She moves up* R. *of the table.*) Which particular film-star are you copying this week ?

BRENT (*crossing between* PHILLIPS *and* JOSEPHINE *to* R. *of the table*). I've been to look at the water. Sister, what will happen if the Great Dyke doesn't hold ? (*She sits in the chair,* R. *of the table.*)

JOSEPHINE (*placing a covered plate on the table, in front of* BRENT). All the villagers will be homeless and crowding up here on the high ground. (*She puts a jug of coffee on the table.*) And where we

shall put them and how we shall feed them, goodness only knows.
(*She puts the tray on the sideboard.*)

BRENT (*opening her table napkin*). Food's no problem to you.
You're a genius. Sister Agnes says you could make creamed chicken
stew out of a diabetic hippopotamus.

JOSEPHINE. Sister Agnes and Nurse Brent have one thing in
common—they talk too much. Eat your supper before you're late
on duty. Good evening, Nurse Phillips. I hope you enjoyed your
meal.

PHILLIPS (*looking up*). I found it completely adequate, thank you,
Sister. (*She returns to her paper.*)

JOSEPHINE. Oh, you did ? Well, I suppose that's something to
be thankful for. (*She lifts the dish-cover and puts it on the sideboard.*)

BRENT. Sister Josephine ! Mushroom omelette and that
heavenly savoury sauce. (*She sniffs at the jug.*) And coffee. (*She
eagerly picks up the knife and fork.*) Honestly, if I stay here long, I
shall get *fat* . . .

JOSEPHINE (L. *of* BRENT). Ah, now—wait a moment.

(BRENT *pauses and looks up at* JOSEPHINE.)

Well ? (*Gently.*) No blessing, child ?

BRENT (*putting down her knife and fork*). Oh, I'm so sorry. (*She
folds her hands.*) Dear Lord, thank you for my most excellent supper
and for making Sister Josephine such a divine cook.

JOSEPHINE (*with a twinkling smile*). Now, now—let us have a
little reverence. (*She prompts quietly.*) *Benedictus* . . .

BRENT. *Benedictus, Benedicat, per Jesum Christum dominum
Nostrum,* Amen. (*She picks up her knife and fork and starts to eat
hungrily.*)

JOSEPHINE (*crossing herself*). Amen. (*Briskly.*) Now savour
every mouthful in the good Lord's name. My word—this wind and
rain. I pity the poor souls on the road tonight. (*She crosses to the
switches above the fireplace and switches on the wall brackets and the
lantern lights.*)

(*The hall is flooded with soft light.*)

(*She crosses to the sideboard.*) I think we should keep the place **extra**
warm just in case. (*She lifts the telephone receiver.*)

BRENT (*speaking with her mouth full*). I believe you *are* expecting
trouble.

JOSEPHINE (*dialling*). You concentrate on your supper. Masticate it now, masticate it. Good food well cooked should be
approached in a spirit of humility and understanding. (*Into the
telephone.*) Sister Agnes, is Willy around ? . . . Would you please
ask him to bring some logs into the hall. I'm going to keep a good
fire in . . . Yes, as well be prepared. (*She replaces the receiver.*)

(PHILLIPS *pushes back her chair, rises, crumples the newspaper and drops
it on the* L. *end of the table.*)

(*She gives almost a little shriek.*)   Nurse Phillips !   (*She moves above* PHILLIPS *to* L. *of the table.*)

PHILLIPS.   Sister—what *is* it ?

JOSEPHINE (*carefully smoothing out the newspaper and folding it flat*).   Haven't I begged you girls to keep all the old newspapers and not to crumple them like that ?

PHILLIPS (*rolling up her table napkin*).   You must have thousands stored.

(BRENT *pours herself a cup of coffee.*)

JOSEPHINE.   Yes, and a thousand and one uses for them.   Never discard a newspaper and never throw away a piece of string.   (*She puts the folded newspaper carefully on the* L. *end of the table, moves to the armchair* L.C., *sits and takes some knitting from her pocket.*)

(PHILLIPS *resumes her seat above the table, opens the book and starts to read.*)

History might have been altered many times if a piece of string or an old newspaper had been lying handy.

BRENT.   Sister Josephine is actually sitting down.   Was it an accident, Sister, or did you just forget ?

JOSEPHINE (*with her twinkling smile*).   No impertinence from you, miss.   I'm only waiting on your dishes.   (*She knits rapidly.*)   I want to finish this for Mrs Thomas.   Poor dear—her leg gets so cold now it isn't there any more.

BRENT.   Sister Mary sat up with her for nearly forty-eight hours. She ought to have died.

JOSEPHINE.   My good girl, if Sister Mary says people are not to die, then they don't die, and that's that.

PHILLIPS (*looking up*).   From a medical and surgical point of view, Mrs Thomas *should* have died.

BRENT.   You sound quite disappointed.   (*She drinks her coffee.*)

PHILLIPS.   Not at all.   But I do like things to be *logical*.   (*She resumes reading.*)

JOSEPHINE.   And so you've no room for miracles.   Well, well, we're all as the good God made us—only He must get a mite puzzled sometimes.

(WILLY PENTRIDGE *enters down* R.   *He is a tall, big, loosely-built youth of uncertain age.   He walks with a very slight stoop and the awkward gait often found in mentally deficient people.   His face is not so much vacant as unresponsive, until he becomes interested, when it changes to an expression of strained and searching eagerness.   He wears blue overalls, a green baize apron and his shirt sleeves are rolled to the elbows.   When he speaks, it is in the wide tones of the Fen country. He carries a basket of logs.*)

Ah, good boy, Willy.   Will you mend the fire, please ?   We're rather shivery.

WILLY (*crossing below the table and the armchair to the fireplace*). Ah, sure-ley. Floods be out. Tes always coold when floods be out.

BRENT. Definitely ? Are they out ?

WILLY (*turning*). Not yet. But yee'll be hearing later right enough. (*He puts the basket down, kneels and carefully builds up the fire.*)

BRENT. I told you he'd know. What's happening, Willy ? What are the people doing ?

WILLY. Bobbin' about wi' lanterns, they are. Like as many ants. And the botes—they're going tew. Some they're makin' for Norwich. But they woon't get there, they woon't. Waters be turrible strong once they're out. (*He rises suddenly and turns.*) Smash a liddle bote in a minute, they will. Smash her into nuthin'. (*With an unexpected movement he claps his big hands together.*)

(PHILLIPS *starts.*)

JOSEPHINE (*placidly*). Now, Willy.

WILLY (*to* JOSEPHINE ; *smiling*). Have yee seen Sister Mary, please ? She promised I some sweeties, she did. Out of the big brass box in her room. I bin polishing it. (*He stoops and takes a log from the basket.*) Shines like the liddle old moon, she does—all ready to have top taken off. (*He puts the log on the fire.*)

PHILLIPS (*looking at* WILLY). Are you sure you haven't taken a few sweets already ?

WILLY (*straightening up*). Why would I do that ?

PHILLIPS. Why not ?

WILLY. Because it's in the wise book that Sister reads. (*He raises his hands and looks at them.*) " Keep they hands from pickin' and stealin.'' (*His face begins to work. He holds his hands out to* JOSEPHINE.) Have my hands been pickin' and stealin ', Sister ?

JOSEPHINE. I'm quite certain they haven't.

WILLY (*crossing to* PHILLIPS). But Nurse here—she says they been pickin' and stealin'.

PHILLIPS. Oh, be *quiet*. And keep them away from my apron. They're filthy.

WILLY. They may be filthy, but they've got no sin on un. (*He looks at his hands, puzzled.*) Least, I can't see none. (*He turns to* JOSEPHINE.) Can you see sin on my hands, Sister ? (*He holds out his hands to her.*) Tell her you can't see no . . .

PHILLIPS (*putting down her book and rising*). Oh, for mercy's sake.

JOSEPHINE (*rising*). Willy, listen to me. (*She puts her knitting in her pocket.*)

WILLY (*suddenly angry*). She's down on me, she is. Why ?

PHILLIPS. Nothing of the kind.

WILLY. I never hurt her. I never hurt the littlest crawling thing. (*He suddenly siezes another log.*)

(*He turns and moves above the* L. *end of the table.*) If I saw anyone hurting anything— (*he towers over* PHILLIPS) I'd crush them—so I would.

(PHILLIPS *cowers away from* WILLY. BRENT *sits staring, her cup halfway to her mouth.* SISTER MARY BONAVENTURE *enters by the Hospital door. She is between thirty-five and forty, tall and beautifully made. Even her plain blue habit is worn with grace. The white-winged cornette sets off the fine clear pink and white of her skin, the lovely breadth of the intelligent forehead, and the gentle but penetrating blue eyes. Her voice is cultured, full and beautiful. She carries a large piece of old faded tapestry over one arm, and has several neatly folded newspapers tucked under her elbow.*)

(*Without taking his eyes off* PHILLIPS *he shouts.*) Crush them like that ! (*He crashes the log down on to the table in front of* PHILLIPS.)

(PHILLIPS *recoils.* BRENT *squeals.* JOSEPHINE *takes a step towards* WILLY.)

MARY (*calling from the gallery*). Willy !

(*They all stop dead. There is a pause and silence.* WILLY *is bent over the table, his hand hard down on the log.*)

(*Quietly.*) Did you forget the words again, Willy ?
WILLY (*without moving*). I—lost 'em, Sister.
MARY. They're in your head. Think now, think carefully. (*She pauses, then prompts gently.*) To everything . . .
WILLY. To everything— (*he lifts his head a little and the light comes slowly back into his face*) there is—to everything there is a—season—season——
MARY. And a time . . .
WILLY (*painfully remembering*) —and a time to every purpose——
MARY. Under . . .
WILLY. —under the heavens. A time to plant—a time to . . . (*He suddenly becomes tense.*) I lost it, Sister—I lost it.
MARY. What comes after planting ?
WILLY. A time to—yes—a time to pluck up that which is to be planted.
MARY (*moving down two steps*). Bravo. That was the hard part. You know the rest.
WILLY (*lifting his head*). A time to kill and a time to heal——
MARY. Yes, Willy—go on.
WILLY. —a time to—break down— (*his head droops again*) and a time to build up. (*With a half sob.*) I'm sorry, Sister.
MARY. Good boy, Willy.
WILLY. Build up. (*He looks at the log.*) Will I build up the fire, Sister ?
MARY. Yes, please.

(WILLY *slowly picks up the log, crosses to the fireplace and busies him-self at it.* PHILLIPS *breaks up* R. MARY *comes quickly and lightly down the stairs, moves to the table and runs her hand across the surface.*)

(*To* WILLY.)   Poor Sister Josephine's polished table.   We'll ask her to give you some oil and a soft rag and then you can put it in order again.

WILLY (*turning*).   And then may I have the sweeties—from the big brass box wi' the eagle on the top ?

MARY.   Get them now.   You know where they are.   You can fix the table after supper.

WILLY.   Yes, Sister.   (*He moves quietly to the stairs, starts up them, then stops, turns, and holds out his hands to* MARY.)   Sister, are my hands clean of sin ?   There's fire dirt here—and that, that's metal polish.   I mean—are they . . . ?

MARY (*in the wide Fen tones*).   Yes, Willy.   Praper clean.

WILLY (*beaming*).   Praper clean.

(*With a triumphant look at* PHILLIPS, *he goes up the stairs and exits up* L.)

MARY (*with a change of voice*).   I have asked you all to use gentle-ness and tact with that poor mind.

JOSEPHINE.   I'm afraid tact is not Nurse Phillips' speciality.

PHILLIPS (*moving above the table*).   I told him his hands were filthy.   Which, of course, they were.

MARY.   And then, Nurse ?

BRENT (*rising*).   I don't think she's entirely to . . .

MARY.   I'm asking Nurse Phillips.

(*The rebuke is quiet and entirely without harshness, but* BRENT *flushes and looks down.*)

BRENT.   Yes, Sister.

MARY.   I see you've finished your supper.   Will you go on duty now, please ?   Read the notes I've left about Mrs Thomas.   Read them carefully.   We shall need your help.

BRENT (*gratified*).   Yes, Sister.   (*She crosses below the table to the fireplace, collects her cape, and hurries to the stairs.*)

(PHILLIPS *picks up her book and puts it on the sideboard.* JOSEPHINE *moves the log basket below the stool down* L.)

MARY (*to* BRENT).   Oh, Nurse.

(BRENT *stops and turns.*)

Your hair is very soft and pretty.   But while you are on duty, I think I should roll it back more neatly.

BRENT.   Yes, Sister.   Thank you, Sister.

(*She goes up the stairs and exits by the Hospital door.* MARY *turns to*
PHILLIPS.)

MARY. Nurse, I want you to remember you can always calm
Willy with words—any words with colour in them. Or even a verse.

PHILLIPS. If you'll forgive my speaking bluntly, Sister, I don't
think he should be allowed so much freedom. He's so quickly
roused, and with that mentality and his muscular strength, he could
quite easily be *very* dangerous.

MARY. That's for us to judge. He's probably better employed
up here than at liberty in the village.

PHILLIPS. But it's a question of . . .

MARY. In this case, of tolerance.

PHILLIPS. Tolerance undermines discipline.

MARY. If you'll forgive my speaking bluntly in turn, Nurse, I
don't think you appreciate the borderline between discipline and
severity.

PHILLIPS. I . . . (*She stands rigidly on her dignity.*)

MARY. I'm sorry you're leaving us. You're an excellent nurse,
and I'm sure you'll make your way in the profession. (*She looks at*
PHILLIPS.) Only—if you could just realize humanity isn't ruled in
straight lines—I think perhaps you would be happier.

PHILLIPS (*stiffly*). Thank you, Sister.

MARY (*ruefully*). I don't mean to preach, you know.

(BRENT *enters by the Hospital door.*)

BRENT (*calling from the gallery ; breathlessly*). Excuse me, Sister
—Nurse Phillips, you're wanted on the phone.

PHILLIPS. *Which* phone ?

(BRENT *looks at* PHILLIPS *pityingly and speaks to her as to a backward
child.*)

BRENT. The *telephone.*

(*She exits by the Hospital door.* PHILLIPS *gives an impatient gesture.*
JOSEPHINE *hides a smile.*)

PHILLIPS. If you'll excuse me, Sister.

MARY. Of course.

(PHILLIPS *moves hurriedly to the stairs, goes up them and exits by the
Hospital door.* MARY *looks after her a moment, then turns to*
JOSEPHINE.)

There goes the potential matron of a State Institution. (*She pauses.
With a sigh.*) She'll run it most efficiently.

JOSEPHINE. With discipline. *Discipline.* A pity she's not staying. You wear them all down in time.

MARY. Not at all. They merely come round to our way of
thinking. (*She laughs.*) We *have* had some tough ones, haven't

we ?   Do you remember the Manchester staff nurse with a passion for diet and an obsession about counting calories ?

JOSEPHINE.   She actually invaded my kitchen.   (*Grimly.*)   I caloried her.   How's Mrs Thomas ?

MARY.   Bonny.   She's sent you down two immaculate copies of *The Times*.   (*She hands the newspapers to* JOSEPHINE.)   I'm to tell you they haven't even been opened.

JOSEPHINE (*crossing to* L. *of the table*).   Bless her heart.   I *do* like *The Times*.   (*She puts the newspapers neatly with the one already on the table.*)   The pages have such a nice even grey effect on my shelves —none of those big untidy headings like the *Daily Express*.

MARY (*hanging the tapestry over the back of the armchair* L.C.).   When you die, Sister Josephine, you'll have newspaper wings.   Look, I brought down that tapestry we found in the old cupboard.

(JOSEPHINE *moves to the sideboard, picks up the tray and dish-cover and puts them on the table.*)

Such a pity—I'm afraid it's past repairing.   (*She pauses, then reels a little, puts one hand to her head and grips the back of the armchair for support.*)

JOSEPHINE (*about to stack the plates*).   Sister Agnes will tackle it.   (*She sees* MARY, *and crosses quickly to her.*)   Here—you'd better sit down.   (*She helps* MARY *to sit in the armchair* L.C.)   Steady now— let me . . .

MARY.   Thank you—just giddiness—it's passing.

JOSEPHINE.   You've had no sleep for nearly two nights.

MARY.   But people are already trickling up from the village, and there's so much to be done.

JOSEPHINE (*moving to the table*).   Then someone else will have to do it for once.   (*She stacks the dirty plates, cups and cutlery on the tray.*)   Even you can't go on for ever.   You promise me to sit here by the fire for a quarter of an hour, and then I'll take a bowl of hot onion soup to your room.   That'll put heart into you.

MARY.   Your onion soup would put heart into a graven image.

JOSEPHINE (*picking up the loaded tray*).   Don't waste it, even in jest.   (*She moves below the table.*)   Why, dear goodness knows it takes enough time and material . . .

(DR JEFFREYS *enters down* R.   *He is a handsome man of thirty-five, normally with great poise and charm.   At the moment he is wet and bedraggled.   He wears a black oilskin and wellington boots.   He carries a sou'wester and a small case.*)

JEFFREYS (*laughing*).   Good evening, Sister Josephine.   Campaigning as usual ?

JOSEPHINE.   Good evening, Doctor.   Tell me—as a medical man, would you consider half an hour's rest a mortal sin ?

JEFFREYS.   I certainly should not.

JOSEPHINE. Then try convincing Sister Bonaventure. (*She rustles below him to the arch down* R.) That'll keep you busy.

(*She exits down* R. JEFFREYS *moves* L. *of the table and places his sou'-wester and case on it.*)

JEFFREYS. That means you haven't been to bed since I left.

MARY. I've had all the rest I need.

JEFFREYS. You've such a spartan idea of your own needs. You can't go on giving yourself like this. I insist you rest.

MARY. But, Doctor . . .

JEFFREYS. No. That's an order—Matron. (*He takes off his oilskins.*)

MARY (*smiling*). Yes—Doctor. Thank you. (*Quietly.*) But aren't *you* making rather a late visit ?

JEFFREYS. I'm staying here ready. That dyke can't possibly hold.

MARY. Apparently we coped with the same thing sixty years ago. We can do it again now.

JEFFREYS. What you mean, Sister, is that you'll cope—and we shall follow.

(*He drapes his oilskins over his arm, picks up his sou'wester and case from the table, goes up the stairs and exits by the Hospital door.* MARY *relaxes in the armchair and slips her rosary through her fingers. The* MOTHER SUPERIOR *enters* L. *She is an older woman than* MARY, *with an air of great authority. The only difference between her habit and that of the others is the large cross on a chain around her neck. She moves quietly to* C., *pauses as she sees* MARY, *then turns to go out again.* MARY *sits up.*)

MARY. I beg your pardon, Reverend Mother. (*She half rises.*)

MOTHER SUPERIOR (*moving* R. *of* MARY). No—don't get up, Sister. I know you're off duty. I just wanted to check with you that we're ready for all emergencies.

MARY. Yes. We've managed to clear those two large wards. We can put the men in one and the women and children in the other when they arrive.

MOTHER SUPERIOR. Good.

MARY. They'll have to camp out for a little, until we get properly organized and they can keep control themselves.

MOTHER SUPERIOR. Sister Agnes is ready at the switchboard for messages. By the way, Willy's mother has come up—their cottage has already gone, I'm afraid. She'll be very helpful. I expect you can find beds for them both.

MARY. Yes, of course.

MOTHER SUPERIOR. And Sister Josephine tells me she has made arrangements for plenty of hot soup.

MARY (*involuntarily*). Onion soup.

MOTHER SUPERIOR (*drily*). Precisely. Onion soup.

(They look at each other and laugh.)

(She moves to the chair above the table and sits.) How very happy she will be officiating. *(She leans forward, folding her hands on the table in front of her. Gravely.)* Life must be quite simple and uncomplicated for the Josephines of this world.

MARY *(quietly)*. Yes.

MOTHER SUPERIOR. You look tired—very tired. I've been watching you for some weeks. When this weather clears, would you care to go into retreat for a little ?

(MARY's hands close hard over the carved arms of the chair. She rises.)

MARY *(turning to the fireplace ; abruptly)*. No—I would not. *(She turns.)* I'm sorry. If you wish to send me away . . .

MOTHER SUPERIOR *(gently)*. How long have you been here ? Six years ?

MARY. Nearly seven.

MOTHER SUPERIOR. We've never had our hospital run so efficiently. No, I don't want to lose you. I only wonder if we haven't lost you already. Spiritually.

MARY *(moving restlessly up* L.C.*)*. I don't—know.

MOTHER SUPERIOR. I'm not trying to force your confidence. But if I can help you . . . *(Quietly.)* What is it, Sister ?

MARY *(turning)*. Just that . . . *(She breaks off, pauses, and moves down* C.*)*

MOTHER SUPERIOR. For you, matters are neither simple nor uncomplicated.

MARY. And why not ? It's merely mental adjustment. If I were studying for an examination, I should will my brain to concentrate. Other things would be excluded—completely.

MOTHER SUPERIOR. And these—other things—are not ?

MARY. No. *(She moves to the fireplace and turns.)* This restlessness—the uncertainty. If one could be sure one had done the right thing.

MOTHER SUPERIOR. We all go through this conflict, you know. Even the Josephines.

MARY. Perhaps they have more balance.

MOTHER SUPERIOR. Or the finer vessel needs longer in the kiln.

MARY. We're put into the world, as the world is, and as we are. Is it wise to leave it—to narrow ourselves into a little space ?

MOTHER SUPERIOR. Do we ? We're a serving Order, not a closed House.

MARY *(turning and gazing into the fire)*. I feel if it were *right*, there should be no question in the mind. Can we ever be sure ? *(She turns.)* Are you sure ?

MOTHER SUPERIOR. At my age, yes. At yours—I can't think I was so certain. Our normal emotions—and desires—aren't sublimated without a struggle. We know that when we take our vows.

MARY. That's the easy part. (*She turns and looks up at the crucifix over the fireplace.*)   I remember the exaltation—an ecstasy almost physical.   (*Slowly.*)   Afterwards—when it became a question of work and routine . . .

MOTHER SUPERIOR (*nodding*).   And loneliness.

MARY (*turning*).   Yes.   The mental loneliness.   And yet, that's something all the saints must have had to bear.

MOTHER SUPERIOR (*rising and moving to* MARY).   My child, saints and martyrs have had their day.   In our time we need practical Christianity.   You'll do more good sitting up with Mrs Thomas than going to the stake in a blaze of righteousness.

(*The doorbell clangs shrilly off* R.)

Believe me, I do understand.   For a woman of your character and knowledge, service—and above all, humility—are not easy.   You're tired and for the moment the world seems stronger than the spirit. It will pass.   I am sure it will pass.

MARY.   Thank you, Reverend Mother.

MOTHER SUPERIOR.   If you want to rest later, it can be arranged. If you are happier working—as I think you are—the work is certainly to hand.

(JOSEPHINE *enters down* R.)

(*She turns.*)   Yes, Sister Josephine ?

JOSEPHINE (*moving* C.).   Reverend Mother, there's a man wanting to speak to you.   They're travelling from London by car—he and two women and a driver.   They're cut off by the floodwater.

MOTHER SUPERIOR.   Will you bring them in, Sister ?   (*To* MARY.) This is probably the first of the rush.

(JOSEPHINE *turns and moves to the arch down* R.)

(*She turns and calls.*)   Sister Josephine.

(JOSEPHINE *stops and turns.*)

(*With a smile.*)   Be ready with your loaves and fishes.

JOSEPHINE (*beaming*).   Yes, Reverend Mother.

(*She exits down* R.)

MOTHER SUPERIOR (*turning to* MARY).   You see ?   No need to look for our work.   Would you be so good as to give Sister Josephine a little assistance ?

MARY.   Yes, Reverend Mother.   (*She crosses to the arch down* R.)

MOTHER SUPERIOR.   Sister——

(MARY *stops and turns.*)

—I'm sure it will be all right.   We need you too badly.

MARY (*smiling*). Don't be too kind to me. I find few things harder to fight than vanity.

(*She exits down* R. *The* MOTHER SUPERIOR *moves to the fireplace and stirs the logs with the poker.* JOSEPHINE *enters down* R.)

JOSEPHINE (*as she enters*). Would ye be pleased to come this way ? (*She stands aside, above the arch.*)

(MELLING *enters down* R. *He is a prison warder, but for the moment, his uniform is concealed under the blue raincoat and white scarf that he wears. He has no hat. He is a spruce, upright man, about forty. His shoes and trouser legs are black with wet.* JOSEPHINE *exits down* R.)

MOTHER SUPERIOR. Good evening—come in. You must be nearly drowned.

MELLING (*moving above the table to* C.). I'm sorry to arrive like this, madam, but we're travelling from London, and I'm afraid the car is waterlogged.

MOTHER SUPERIOR. We shall have many people coming here to the high ground tonight. Come to the fire. (*She pauses.*) But I thought you had others with you ?

MELLING. Yes. (*He pauses, then turns towards the arch down* R. *and calls.*) Come in.

(SARAT CARN *enters down* R., *followed by* MISS PIERCE. SARAT *is tall. Her eyes are magnificent and even at this unfavourable moment there is a kind of fierce magnetism about her. She wears a long travelling dress of dull crimson cloth and a caped coat of the same material is flung across her shoulders, cloak fashion. She has no handbag. She walks with a long sweeping stride. She pauses a moment in the arch, then moves* C. MISS PIERCE *stands* R. *below the arch. She is a prison wardress and wears an inconspicuous navy blue uniform tunic and skirt, a shirt-blouse and tie, brown leather gloves and a navy blue woollen scarf around her throat and across one shoulder. She has no hat. She is an upright, pleasant-looking woman about thirty-two or three and might be taken for a governess or a good-class lady's maid. The* MOTHER SUPERIOR *hurries forward and meets* SARAT *at* C.)

MOTHER SUPERIOR. Come in—why, you look positively exhausted. Are you ill ? (*She puts out a hand.*)

SARAT (*drawing herself up ; abruptly*). No.

(*The* MOTHER SUPERIOR *draws back, puzzled.*)

No—I'm not ill, thank you. (*She crosses below the* MOTHER SUPERIOR *to* L., *walking steadily, her coat held tightly round her.*) If I might sit by your fire.

MOTHER SUPERIOR. But certainly. (*She moves to* SARAT *to take the wet coat from her shoulders.*) They haven't taken your wet coat.

SARAT (*abruptly*). Leave it, please. (*She sits in the armchair* L.C., *and shivers slightly as she holds her hands to the blaze.*)

PIERCE (*quickly*). We're very grateful to you. (*She crosses to the fireplace.*) I hope we're not disorganizing things. (*She takes off her gloves.*)

MOTHER SUPERIOR. Not at all. One of our Sisters is getting you something hot. (*She glances at* SARAT.) Are you sure your . . .

MELLING. Madam, could I have a word with you in private, if you please ?

MOTHER SUPERIOR (*turning to* MELLING). Do sit down. I assure you we're quite private here.

MELLING (*respectfully*). I think I ought to speak to you quite alone, madam—if you don't mind.

(*The* MOTHER SUPERIOR *looks at* MELLING, *then at* SARAT. *She nods.*)

MOTHER SUPERIOR (*moving to the door* L.). Will you come with me ?

(*She exits* L., *followed by* MELLING. SARAT *leans back wearily in the chair.* PIERCE *sits quietly on the stool down* L., *loosens her scarf, takes off her shoes and stockings, places the stockings in the hearth, then puts her shoes on again.*)

PIERCE. I should take yours off, too. You'll get a chill.

SARAT (*harshly*). That would be very inconvenient, wouldn't it ? Think how the calendar would be thrown out.

PIERCE. Please—it won't help to be . . .

SARAT. In fact, the whole thing is very humorous. A convent of all places. The holy woman is going to get an unpleasant shock in a few minutes.

(PIERCE *rises, puts her gloves on the stool, and moves to* L. *of* SARAT.)

PIERCE. That coat is soaked. (*She lays a hand on* SARAT'S *shoulder.*) Let me . . .

SARAT (*fiercely*). Take your hands off me. I've told you that before.

PIERCE (*quietly*). Don't be difficult.

SARAT. It's my privilege to be what I can while I can. And get away from me. There's plenty of space here. Get away, please—right away.

PIERCE (*shrugging her shoulders*). Very well. (*She moves above the armchair, then up* R.)

(SARAT, *without looking round, snaps her fingers over the side of the chair.*)

SARAT. No, no—don't leave the fire. I didn't mean that. I don't want you to be cold and wretched. If you would just sit—where I can't see you.

(PIERCE *moves quietly to the chair above the table and sits.*)

(*She does not look at* PIERCE.)　Are you all right there ?

PIERCE.　Yes, thank you.

(*There is a pause.*　SARAT *leans back and stares at the ceiling.*)

SARAT.　Do you know this place ?

PIERCE.　Yes.

SARAT.　How far from—Norwich ?

PIERCE.　About fifteen miles.

SARAT.　Fifteen.　(*Abruptly.*)　How far are we from Denzil St David ?

PIERCE.　Not more than two miles.

SARAT.　I thought so when the holy woman mentioned the high ground.　The journey has been so confused in the dark and flood-water.　So *this* is Our Lady of Rheims ?

PIERCE.　Yes.

SARAT.　I told you it was funny, didn't I ?　(*She laughs almost hysterically.*)

PIERCE (*rising quickly and moving* C. ; *sharply*).　Now, please !

(SARAT *abruptly stops laughing.*)

SARAT.　All right.　I've not been hysterical so far, have I ?

PIERCE.　You've behaved very well.　Very well indeed.

SARAT.　Then you've nothing to worry about.　So be quiet and leave me alone.

(MARY *enters down* R.　*She carries two bowls of hot soup on a tray.*)

MARY (*moving below the table*).　I'm sorry to keep you waiting. You must be very chilled.　(*She places the tray on the table.*)　I can recommend this very excellent soup.　Some of us think our cook has missed her vocation.

PIERCE (*sitting above the table*).　It looks and smells wonderful.

MARY (*placing a bowl of soup and a spoon in front of* PIERCE).　It tastes better.　(*To* SARAT.)　Will you come to the table, or would you like it there by the fire ?

(SARAT *does not answer.*)

PIERCE (*rising*).　I'll take it to her.

MARY.　No, no.　Sit down and drink yours while it's nice and hot.

(PIERCE *sits and starts to drink her soup, watching* SARAT *and* MARY *carefully as she does so.*)

(*She picks up a bowl of soup and a spoon and moves to* R. *of* SARAT.) Why—that wet coat—you poor child.　(*She turns to the table, puts the soup and spoon down, then moves again to* R. *of* SARAT.)

(SARAT *turns her head and they face each other.*　MARY *draws a sudden quick breath.　There is a pause, then* SARAT *turns her head away.*)

(Gently.) Do let me take that coat.   You see—it's spoiling our piece
of tapestry.

SARAT.   You could take it away, couldn't you ?

MARY.   It's convenient there.   It stops the draught from the
staircase.

(SARAT *looks at* MARY *again.   Then very slowly she rises and slips off
her coat.*   MARY *takes it and spreads it over the stool down* L. *to
dry.*)

SARAT.   And my wet shoes—are they spoiling your hearthrug ?

MARY.   No.   But they can't be very comfortable.   Won't you
take them off ?

(*With a little shrug,* SARAT *sits in the armchair and bends down to her
shoes.*)

Let me.   (*She kneels in front of* SARAT.)

SARAT (*drawing her feet under her ; fiercely*).   No—get up.   Get
up at once.

MARY.   But why . . . ?

SARAT (*urgently*).   Get off your knees—in front of me.

(*She rises desperately and turns up* C.   PIERCE *rises quickly and
intercepts her.*)

PIERCE (*firmly, but not unkindly*).   Now steady—take a grip on
yourself.

SARAT (*thrusting her off ; desperately, under her breath*).   Leave me
alone—leave me alone.   (*She moves to the pillar up* R. *and stands with
one hand against it, her head bent and her back to the audience.*)

(MARY *rises.*)

PIERCE (*moving quickly to* MARY).   I beg your pardon, Sister.
She's a little upset.

MARY.   She must be ill.

PIERCE (*quietly*).   She's not ill.   Just take no notice.

MARY.   Is there nothing . . . ?

PIERCE.   Nothing that you or I can do anything about.

MARY.   I felt when I spoke to her . . .

PIERCE.   I thought perhaps you knew her.

MARY.   I've never seen her before.   But there must be something
terribly wrong.   She isn't . . . ?

PIERCE.   She is neither ill nor insane.   Believe me, Sister, the
best way you can help is to be normal.

MARY.   If you assure me . . .

PIERCE.   It is the only thing.   (*She moves to the chair above the
table, sits, and gets on with her soup.*)

MARY.   Very well.   (*She moves to* SARAT.)

(PIERCE *watches warily.*)

(*To* SARAT.) Won't you at least come back to the fire ?

(SARAT *does not answer for a second, then she turns and moves to the fireplace.*)

(*She moves to the table, picks up the bowl of soup and spoon, and takes it to* SARAT.) And have some hot soup to warm you ? (*She holds out the bowl.*)

(SARAT *takes the bowl and spoon, then sits in the armchair* L.C.)

(*She smiles triumphantly at* PIERCE. *To* SARAT.) That's better. Thank you for humouring me. Now I'll see if I can find you both some slippers. (*She moves to the stairs.*)

(SARAT *drinks a spoonful or two of soup.*)

PIERCE. You're very good, Sister, but don't bother. As soon as we can we must be on our way to Norwich.

MARY (*stopping on the stairs and turning*). I'm afraid you won't get to Norwich tonight. It wouldn't be safe to try. The Great Dyke may give way at any time unless the men achieve a miracle of engineering.

(SARAT *turns in her chair.* PIERCE *rises.*)

SARAT (*slowly*). Then—we might be here for some time ?
MARY. Some days, perhaps.

(*She goes up the stairs and exits by the Hospital door.*)

SARAT. Do you hear that, Pierce ?
PIERCE (*resuming her seat ; noncommittally*). Yes. (*She finishes her soup.*)
SARAT. Do you remember what I said about the calendar ?
PIERCE. Try and be sensible. Don't bank on it.
SARAT. Why not ? Isn't there a trite saying about drowning men and straws ? Except that I'm not—drowning.
PIERCE. It looks as if we've only just escaped it.
SARAT. What a pity.

(MARY *enters by the Hospital door and comes down the stairs.*)

MARY (*moving* C.). One of our nurses is getting you some shoes.
PIERCE. Thank you very much.
SARAT. You were right about the soup. My compliments to your cook—for what they're worth. (*She holds out the bowl and spoon to* MARY.)
MARY (*laughing*). She'll be delighted. Nothing pleases her more than to have her work appreciated. (*She takes the bowl and spoon.*) Only—you haven't had very much.

(PIERCE *rises and eases up* R.)

SARAT. All I wanted, thank you.

(MARY *puts the bowl and spoon on the table.*)

(*She rises, goes to her coat, takes a packet of cigarettes from her pocket, is about to take a cigarette, then pauses.*) Oh, I'm sorry. I suppose it isn't permitted to smoke in here.

MARY. Not usually. But in these circumstances . . .

SARAT (*moving* C. ; *abruptly*). What circumstances ?

MARY. But surely . . .

SARAT (*sharply*). I said—what circumstances ?

PIERCE (*warningly*). Careful.

MARY. I meant that—soon this place must be free to all, and we shan't be so strict about regulations. So if you would like to smoke . . . (*She takes a box of matches from the table, lights one and holds it out.*)

(SARAT *looks at* MARY, *then lights her cigarette.*)

SARAT (*crossing below* MARY *to* L. *of* PIERCE). You're a good woman.

(MARY *moves to the fireplace, throws the spent match into the fire, then picks up* SARAT'S *coat and holds it up in the front of the fire to dry.*)

(*To* PIERCE.) Any good offering you one, Pierce ?

PIERCE. No, thank you.

(SARAT *turns away with a slight shrug, sees* MARY *with the coat and moves quickly to her.*)

SARAT (*taking the coat from* MARY). That must be dry now. I'd like to have it. (*She throws it around her shoulders.*)

MARY. Is that wise ?

SARAT. No, but I'd like to have it. (*She huddles it around her and sits in the armchair* L.C.) It's not wet enough to harm your chair. (*She puts the packet of cigarettes in her pocket, leans back and blows out a cloud of smoke.*)

(BRENT *enters by the Hospital door and clatters down the stairs. She carries a newspaper and two pairs of black shoes.*)

BRENT (*moving* C. ; *breathlessly*). Please, Sister—I've brought the shoes.

MARY (*moving to* L. *of* BRENT). Thank you, Nurse.

BRENT. Two pairs—one from me and one from Nurse Daly. And there's a copy of the local paper for Sister Josephine—old Mr Jenkins in the end ward sent it because it's so nice and smooth. (*She gives the shoes to* MARY, *places the newspaper on the table and smiles happily across at* SARAT.)

MARY. Yes, thank you both very much. Get back to the ward or you'll have Nurse Phillips after you. (*She gives one pair of shoes to* SARAT.)

(BRENT *moves to the stairs and clatters noisily up them.*)

(*She turns. With a smile.*) Quietly, Nurse, quietly! How is Mrs Thomas ?

(SARAT *changes her shoes.*)

BRENT (*stopping, turning and tiptoeing down the stairs*).   In a lovely sleep, Sister.   But Nurse Phillips says she doesn't like the look of Mrs Grimes.   She thinks the baby may come tonight.

MARY.   By the way, have you done any maternity work before ?

BRENT.   Not practical.

MARY.   Then it will be very interesting and good for you.

BRENT (*in a sudden panic*).   Oh-h-h !

MARY.   No—don't get excited.   Just help Nurse Phillips and the doctor.

BRENT (*excitedly*).   Yes, Sister.   Thank you very much.

(*She turns, rushes up the stairs with a clatter and exits by the Hospital door.*)

MARY (*moving to* PIERCE *and giving her the second pair of shoes*). They're not very elegant, but at least they're dry.

PIERCE (*taking the shoes*).   That's the main thing.   (*She moves to the chest up* R., *sits and changes her shoes.*)

(MARY *moves to the table.   She looks at* SARAT.   SARAT *straightens up and meets her glance.*   MARY *collects the bowls and spoons and puts them on the tray.*   SARAT *looks into the fire.*)

SARAT.   Do you arrange everything here ?

MARY.   I'm in charge of the hospital.   We each have our own duties.

SARAT.   Life must be very calm and pleasant.

MARY (*quietly*).   Yes.

SARAT.   Out of the world and away from temptation.

MARY.   I believe that is the popular conception.

SARAT.   How does it really work ?

MARY (*smiling*).   In work.   (*She picks up the tray.*)

SARAT.   No doubt you are filled with a sense of spiritual well-being.   But—are you happy ?

(MARY *glances over her shoulder at* PIERCE, *then puts the tray on the table and moves to* R. *of* SARAT.)

MARY (*deliberately*).   Are you ?

SARAT (*flinching back into the chair ; quietly*).   Oh, God !

MARY (*kneeling beside* SARAT).   Oh, my dear, you can trust me. Won't you tell me what is wrong ?

SARAT.   No—please don't ask—I can't . . .

(*There is a burst of shouting off, a confused noise of raised voices and hurrying feet.   The telephone begins to ring.*   MARY, PIERCE *and* SARAT *rise.*   WILLY *enters suddenly up* L., *and runs down the stairs.*)

WILLY (*as he enters ; shouting at the top of his voice*). Sister—Sister—the Big Dyke's gone—they just sent word—they're leaving the village—I got to ring the great bell—Reverend Mother says to ring the warning bell.

MARY (*intercepting* WILLY *at* C.). Willy—calm yourself.

WILLY (*unheedingly*). I got to ring him loud and clear to warn the people. (*Shouting.*) The floods be out !

(*He dashes to the arch down* R. *and exits.*)

(*He calls wildly. Off.*) The floods be out !

(MARY *crosses to the telephone.*)

PIERCE (*moving above the armchair* L.C.). Can I do anything ?

MARY (*lifting the receiver*). No, we're prepared. (*Into the telephone.*) Yes, Sister Agnes ?... Yes... Ring through to Norwich and let them know ... What ? ... Well, we all know what to do ... Thank you. (*She replaces the receiver.*)

(*The* MOTHER SUPERIOR *and* MELLING *enter* L. *The* MOTHER SUPERIOR *moves above the table to* MARY. MELLING *moves to* L. *of* PIERCE.)

MELLING. Miss Pierce—we can't get away tonight. We shall have to telephone ...

MARY. There's no outside communication. (*To the* MOTHER SUPERIOR.) Sister Agnes has just told me the wires are down.

(JEFFREYS *enters by the Hospital door and hurries down the stairs. He is coatless, his shirt sleeves are rolled up and his hair is damp about his face.*)

JEFFREYS (*moving* C. ; *urgently*). Sister—Sister Mary—can you come ?—the Dyke's gone—they're bringing in the casualties—why didn't the fools give up the attempt before ... (*He breaks off, follows* MARY'S *look, turns and sees* SARAT.) Sarat ! Good God—Sarat !

(SARAT *begins to laugh.* MELLING *moves quickly to* SARAT'S *left and* PIERCE *quickly to* SARAT'S *right.* MARY *moves below the table to* C. SARAT *stops laughing abruptly.*)

MELLING. Now, now, Miss Carn !

MARY (*suddenly*). Sarat—Carn !

SARAT (*defiantly*). Yes, that's my name. Does it mean anything to you ? Think, Sister. Sarat Carn.

PIERCE (*taking hold of* SARAT'S *right arm*). Shall we go outside ?

MOTHER SUPERIOR. You'll have to know, Sister. I'm afraid it will distress you.

(SARAT *takes a step or two towards* MARY. PIERCE *and* MELLING *quickly take her arms and hold them firmly.*)

SARAT. If she's to know, I'll tell her myself.

MELLING. Now come with us, there's a good girl.

SARAT. Be quiet. (*To* MARY. *Without emotion.*) My name is Sarat Carn. Three weeks ago I was tried and convicted for the murder of my brother. We have just come back from London from hearing the appeal. It has been dismissed.

MARY *stands looking at* SARAT. *The* MOTHER SUPERIOR *involuntarily crosses herself. The noise outside rises to full pitch. The great bell of the Convent booms out overhead as—*

the CURTAIN *falls quickly.*

ACT II

SCENE 1

Scene.—SISTER MARY'S *room. Two hours later.*
  The room is in the Hospital section of the Convent. It is a small apartment, the walls built of plain stone as in the Great Hall. Down R., *there is a large window in a pointed arch recess, overlooking an expanse of cold blue-grey sky and a vista of flooded countryside. The window is fitted with a cushioned window seat. An iron slow-combustion stove stands in a low curved arch recess* R.C. *of the back wall. There is a large arched recess in the wall* L. *of the fireplace with a door leading out of the back of it into a small cell-like bedroom. A heavy door down* L. *leads to the main corridor. Above the window* R. *there is a well-filled bookcase with cupboards under it. A big knee-hole desk stands at an angle* R.C. *The desk is very neat and workmanlike, with inkstand, letter tray, blotter, files, etc. A telephone stands at the* R. *end of it, and there is a waste-paper basket underneath it. Two stools stand, one down* R. *and one* L. *of the door up* L.C. *There is an upright chair behind the desk. A bright rush mat lies below the stove. An ebony crucifix hangs over the stove recess. The room is lit by two wall electric candle brackets, one below the door* L. *and the other over the bookcase.*

  (*See the Ground Plan*)

  When the CURTAIN *rises, the lights are lit and a bright fire burns in the stove.* JOSEPHINE *is standing* R. *arranging some daffodils in a vase on the desk. The piece of tapestry is on the stool up* L., *and* MELLING'S *uniform jacket lies on top of it. After a moment,* WILLY *enters* L. *He is still in overalls and carries a large roll of bedding and pillows.*

WILLY. Where do yee want this, Sister ?

(MARTHA PENTRIDGE *enters* L. *She is a gaunt elderly woman. She wears a flowered print overall over a grey dress, with a high collar pinned by a cameo brooch. Her grey hair is drawn back into an uncompromising bun. She carries a white counterpane over her arm.*)

MARTHA (*as she enters ; to* WILLY). In the bedroom, of course, you gurt goop. Where else ?
  WILLY. There's beds all over everywhere at the moment—even in the Chapel—and I were talking to Sister Josephine, I were—so there.

  (*He exits defiantly with his burden up* L.C.)

23

MARTHA (*calling after* WILLY). I'll come about and box yere ears in tew minutes if you're not careful, so I will.

WILLY (*off ; calling*). And what I would be doin' to let yee, I'd like to know.

(MARTHA *moves to the door up* L.C.)

JOSEPHINE. Not now, Martha. You really haven't time.

MARTHA (*moving to* L. *of the desk*). That boy's got above himself since he came to work here. I still think it's a pity they wouldn't take him in the army. (*She nods towards the flowers.*) Those look nice, I must say. Poor Miss Carn. Praper struck I was when I knew she were 'ere.

JOSEPHINE. I suppose it's all over the Convent by now.

MARTHA. Wi' best part of three villages up 'ere together, I don't see 'ow you can stop gossip. Not that I don't know 'ow to guard my own tongue, but seeing I was 'er 'ousekeeper *and* a chief witness, I reckon at least I'm *qualified* to speak.

JOSEPHINE. I know that, Martha. (*She puts the flowers on the bookcase.*) We merely want you to be discreet.

MARTHA (*sniffing*). Which I must say I know 'ow.

(WILLY *enters up* L.C.)

WILLY. I put them two liddle beds up, but these old sheets they got themselves tied round the legs somehow.

(*He exits up* L.C.)

MARTHA (*exasperatedly*). Mercy on us, boy, don't you go trying to make beds. (*She moves to the door up* L.C.) You'll end up wi' yourself tucked in.

(*She exits up* L.C. MARY *enters* L. *at the same time. She carries four small black notebooks.*)

MARY (*moving above the desk*). Thank you, Sister Josephine. (*She looks at the flowers.*) They do look nice.

JOSEPHINE (*crossing to the door up* L.C.). They're bonny, aren't they ?

(MELLING *enters* L. *He is very spick-and-span. He is without his jacket and has his white shirt sleeves neatly rolled. He carries a wicker armchair. He is followed on by the* MOTHER SUPERIOR.)

MOTHER SUPERIOR. Over by the stove, I think, Officer, please.

MELLING (*briskly*). Over by the stove it is. (*To* JOSEPHINE.) Mind your back there, ma'am, thank you.

(JOSEPHINE *moves up* L.C. MELLING *places the chair* R. *of the stove.* JOSEPHINE *exits* L. MARY *places her books on the desk.*)

MOTHER SUPERIOR (*easing* L.C. ; *to* MELLING). Willy has put another bed in there for Miss Pierce. Can you manage with the bunk in the Hall ? And your chauffeur, Mr—Newlands, isn't it ?

MELLING (*moving* R. *of the* MOTHER SUPERIOR). Thank you. I'm hoping it won't be more than a few days—particularly if the telephones are repaired. Meantime, you ladies do understand Miss Carn mustn't be left. Either Miss Pierce, or myself, must be with her, day and night.

MOTHER SUPERIOR. Yes, Officer. But this is Sister Mary's office, and she'll be in here most of the time she's off duty. You've no objection ?

MELLING. Certainly not. Does anyone else come in here during the day ?

MOTHER SUPERIOR. Dr Jeffreys—chiefly during the morning. He's attached to our hospital.

MELLING. We'll take Miss Carn inside when he comes. You see, it's rather unfortunate—he was chief witness for the prosecution.

MOTHER SUPERIOR. Perhaps we can make some other arrangement ?

MARY. This room is the most isolated—at the end of a corridor. And near the long gallery—for exercise.

MELLING. We'll manage fine. Don't put yourselves out any more. And you must let Newlands and me help in any way we can while we're here. (*To the* MOTHER SUPERIOR.) You said there's another chair to be brought along. (*He crosses below her to the door* L.)

MOTHER SUPERIOR. Yes. In the small room off the main hall. I'll come down in a moment and show you.

MELLING. Thank you, madam.

(*He exits* L.)

MOTHER SUPERIOR (*moving to* L. *of the desk*). This means close contact for you. (*Gently.*) That's what you want, isn't it ?

MARY. Yes.

MOTHER SUPERIOR. You needn't—crucify yourself.

MARY. What about her ? It's pitiful. This should be the time for us to offer something—and we're helpless . . .

MOTHER SUPERIOR (*interrupting*). Just a moment, Sister. (*Gently.*) I know our compassion is roused very strongly—but there is one other person we mustn't forget.

(MARY *looks at her.*)

(*Quietly.*) The brother.

MARY. Of course.

MOTHER SUPERIOR (*moving to the door* L.). It might be as well to remember that.

(*She exits.* MARY *sits at the desk, draws a folder of papers towards her, and begins to write. The telephone rings. She lifts the receiver.*)

MARY (*into the telephone*).   Sister Bonaventure... Yes, Doctor, I have them here ... Ask Sister Josephine to bring you some coffee up here, and I'll do them while you wait.   (*She replaces the receiver.*)

(MELLING *enters* L.   *He carries another wicker armchair.*)

MELLING (*cheerfully*).   Shall I put this opposite the other one, madam?

MARY (*indicating a position* L. *of the desk*).   No, here, please, Officer—by the desk.

MELLING (*moving* L. *of the desk*).   Yes, madam.   (*He puts the chair down, then moves to the stool up* L., *picks up his jacket, puts it on and buttons it up.*)

MARY.   Officer.

MELLING (*easing* C.).   Yes, madam?

MARY.   I have specially asked for my room to be put at your disposal because I want to be in touch with Miss Carn—I may be able to bring her a little comfort.

MELLING.   The Reverend Mother gave me to understand that.

MARY.   Is there anything I ought to know?

MELLING.   One thing I should ask you, madam.   I hope you won't encourage the prisoner to any form of self-pity.   It makes things so much harder if they're difficult.

MARY.   Would you say Miss Carn was difficult?

MELLING.   Not more than most, madam, and not so much as some.   Of course, the worst time comes *after* the appeal.

MARY.   And once that's turned down, there's only the Home Secretary.

MELLING.   I must emphatically ask you not to discuss that.   It's most unwise at this stage.   (*Slowly.*)   They all have the same idea, you see.

MARY.   The same idea?

MELLING.   That they're not guilty.

MARY.   And Miss Carn has this—impression—too?

MELLING.   Oh, yes, madam.   Mind you, she doesn't harp on it. She's one of the quiet ones.   In a way, I'm sorry.

MARY.   You think the quiet ones feel it most?

MELLING.   They're most apt to go to pieces at the last moment. (*He turns and moves to the door* L.)

MARY.   I—see.   Will you and Miss Pierce be with her now until ...?

(MELLING *pauses with his hand on the door knob.*)

MELLING.   I shall.   Miss Pierce leaves her when the Chaplain comes.   (*He opens the door.*)

MARY.   Officer—apart from the prison Chaplain—is she allowed to have her own religious adviser?

MELLING.   Yes—but she's expressed no ideas on the subject and doesn't regard the Chaplain very kindly.

MARY. Is a Sister of Mercy allowed to be present ?

MELLING. Madam . . .

MARY. No—no. Up to the time Miss Pierce leaves ?

(MELLING *closes the door and moves* c.)

MELLING. I should forget that idea. This isn't a pretty business for a lady like you.

MARY. Don't be misled by my habit, Officer. I'm a trained nurse. Death is not strange to me.

MELLING. This is a little—different, madam.

MARY. Yes. It can't be very—happy—for you.

MELLING. It's over very quickly.

MARY. How long ?

MELLING. About three minutes from the time the Chaplain comes in.

MARY. Three minutes.

MELLING (*moving to* L. *of the desk*). Perhaps it would be better if I didn't answer any more questions.

MARY. That's a very courteous way of warning me not to ask any.

MELLING. Yes, madam.

MARY. Please call me Sister. But you see—if I don't know the facts, I can't help her.

MELLING. I'm afraid you'll find the approach difficult. Miss Carn isn't quite the usual run of things.

MARY. In what way ?

MELLING. She's an artist, and that means temperament. Did you know she was an artist ?

MARY. Yes.

MELLING. Was doing very well, I understand. Now, if you'll excuse me, Sister, I'll go and give Newlands a hand with those dormitory partitions. (*He turns.*)

(*As he does so,* MARTHA *enters briskly up* L.C.)

MARY. Officer.

(MELLING *pauses.*)

MARTHA. That's nearabout straight, Sister—time Willy's tightened them castors . . .

MARY. Just a moment, Martha, please.

(MARTHA *turns and exits up* L.C.)

MELLING. Yes, Sister ?

MARY. What is your own opinion of the verdict ?

MELLING. The jury were only out fifteen minutes.

MARY. I'm not asking you as an official, Officer.

MELLING. I'd rather you didn't ask me at all. You see—there

are some you feel are the type to do it, and others—well, it's not
so easy to believe.

MARY (*quietly*). And when all is said and done—only Almighty
God ever knows the truth.

MELLING (*moving to the door* L.). He and one other, Sister.

MARY. One other ?

MELLING. The prisoner.

(*He exits* L. MARY *rises, turns to the window* R., *and stands gazing
out.* MARTHA *enters up* L.C.)

MARY (*turning*). Martha—you were Miss Carn's housekeeper,
weren't you ?

MARTHA (*easing* C.). Ar, sure-ley. Right from the time she came
to the village to do them big wall paintings for the church. We were
at the Grape House—the big cottage over to Denzil St David.

MARY. Mr Fenning's old place ? Yes, I know. (*She sits on the
window seat.*)

MARTHA. Took a good lease of it, she did, along wi' old barn
next door. Willy fixed that up for her like it were a praper painting
place.

MARY. And did you—get on with her ? You never found her
difficult ?

MARTHA. Up like the rocket and down like the stick, but leave
her be and she'd mind her own business and yours tew, sweet as any
bird. We were fine till Mr Jason came along.

MARY. Mr Jason ? That was her brother ?

MARTHA. It were all in the papers in full, Sister—pages. Didn't
you read it ?

MARY. No. (*She rises and moves above the desk.*) Tell me
about Mr Jason.

(MARTHA *sits in the chair* L. *of the desk, quite ready to gossip.*)

MARTHA. Well, we'd been settled about a month and he walked
in on us at breakfast one morning, all smiles and as cool as you
please. And I tell you, Sister, the look she guv him was like she
could 'ave struk him to stone on the spot.

MARY. He wasn't a very—likeable—young man ?

MARTHA. Likeable ? Vicious bad, he was, and no mistake. I'd
have said his death were a praper blessing if it hadn't been for poor
Miss Carn.

MARY. So you think she was responsible ?

MARTHA (*rising ; defensively*). I never said that, Sister. And
what's more, I never said it in court neither. But by the time that
lawyer gentleman had done askin' me questions, you'd have thought
I'd seen her do it wi' my own eyes and was standing up there to tell
'em so. (*She pauses, then suddenly resumes her seat.*) Sister—that
was a turrible moment. (*She clasps her hands on her knees and her
head droops.*)

MARY. Giving evidence ?

MARTHA. No. When the Judge put on that liddle black cap and spoke the words. Do you know the words, Sister ?

MARY (*gently*). Yes, Martha, I do.

MARTHA (*very low*). I never looked up, Sister. I never looked up till I knew they'd taken her away.

MARY (*sitting at the desk*). You were called for the Crown, Martha. You had to answer their questions.

MARTHA (*looking up*). The lawyer gentleman said only to tell them what they asked and no more. Well, there was some things they never *asked*, so I never *told* 'em.

MARY. Maybe there was something you should have told them.

MARTHA. I don't suppose it were important. Just some *funny words* I overheard her say one night when he'd been rowing 'er worse'n usual.

MARY. I expect you had a good memory, then, Martha.

MARTHA. What's wrong wi' it now ? I can hear her this minute, plain as plain. It were the word " royal " as struck me.

MARY. Royal ?

MARTHA. She said : " I should have thought that royal affair in Florida would have been a lesson to you." That's what she said. (*Caustically.*) Sounded like he'd been playing round in 'igher circles than usual.

(WILLY *enters up* L.C.)

WILLY (*moving* C.). Sister, I fixed them castors.

MARTHA (*rising and turning*). Now then, big-ears—don't stand idle. Get and fill that stove for Sister.

(SARAT, *followed by* PIERCE, *enters* L. SARAT *wears her coat.*)

PIERCE (*as she enters*). We can take another turn later.

(SARAT *and* PIERCE *stop.* WILLY *turns and stares for a moment at* SARAT.)

WILLY (*moving forward eagerly to* SARAT). Why, it's Miss Sarat.

MARTHA (*moving quickly to* WILLY). Now, Willy . . .

WILLY. Miss Sarat, I am that glad—I praper missed you. When are you comin' back to the Grape House ?

MARTHA (*easing below the others to the door* L.). Come on, Willy.

MARY. Willy, you haven't had any sweets this morning. Get the brass box.

WILLY (*turning ; gleefully*). Yes, Sister. (*He moves quickly to the bookcase, picks up the brass box, puts it on the* L. *end of the desk, opens it and picks over the sweets, talking all the time.*) I could just do wi' one right now—one of them big green ones that tastes like cinnamon—tes the dust I bin pickin' up.

MARTHA. Willy !

WILLY. Would yee like one tew, Miss Sarat ?   Sister wouldn't
mind.

SARAT. No, thank you.

MARY. Take a little lump, Willy, and go with Martha. (*She
resumes her writing.*)

WILLY (*taking several congealed sweets from the box*). Yes, Sister.
(*He crosses below* SARAT *and* PIERCE *to the door* L.)   Good-bye, Miss
Sarat.   I'll see you again when I make up the stove. (*He shows her
the sweets.   Confidentially.*)   I get two or three when they're stuck,
see ?

(MARTHA *pulls* WILLY *to the door* L., *and he exits.*)

MARTHA. I'm that sorry, Miss Sarat.   He just dassn't understand.

(*She exits* L.   SARAT *moves to the stove.*)

PIERCE (*easing up* L.C.).   Melling can look after the stove—then he
needn't come in here again.

SARAT. I don't see why not.

PIERCE. Surely you think . . .

SARAT (*curtly*).   You don't know what I think, Pierce.   It might
be as well for your peace of mind if you don't try. (*She moves restlessly above the desk to the window* R.)

(PIERCE *moves to the chair* R. *of the stove and sits.*   MARY *continues to
write.*)

(*To* MARY.)   Are these your rooms ?

MARY (*without looking up*).   Yes.

SARAT. And you've given them up to us. (*She looks around.*)
It's very—comforting—with the warmth—and the flowers.

MARY. I'm glad you like it.

SARAT (*pacing with long-swinging strides to* L.).   Spacious, too.
One can move around. (*She moves to the door up* L.C.)   Is this the
bedroom ?

MARY. Yes.

(SARAT *opens the door up* L.C., *glances off, then shuts the door and
moves* C.)

SARAT. Whom do I know here beside Martha and Willy ?

MARY. Dr Jeffreys.

SARAT. Oh.   Does he use this room ?

MARY. Occasionally.   But if you'd rather . . . ?

SARAT. Don't worry.   I can go inside.   Not having visitors for a
couple of months has made me rather unsociable, hasn't it, Pierce ?

PIERCE (*reasonably*).   You could have had visitors—and flowers.

SARAT. No, thank you.   The wrong atmosphere for both. (*She
takes a packet of cigarettes from her pocket, then pauses and looks at
MARY.*)

MARY (*glancing up*).   Dr Jeffreys often smokes in here.

SARAT.   Thank you.   (*She takes a cigarette from the packet, returns the packet to her pocket and feels unsuccessfully for matches.*)

(*Without looking up,* MARY *takes a box of matches from a drawer in the desk, places it on the* L. *end of the desk, then resumes writing.*)

(*She lights her cigarette, replaces the matches on the desk, puts the spent match carefully in the ashtray, then paces up* L., *leans against the wall above the door* L., *and smokes for some moments in silence.   To* PIERCE.) Can you blow smoke rings, Pierce ?

PIERCE.   Only by accident.

SARAT.   One often does one's best work by accident.   Sometimes when I'm painting . . .

(*There is a knock at the door* L.)

MARY (*looking up and calling*).   Who is it ?

JEFFREYS (*off* L. ; *calling*).   Jeffreys, Sister.

(MARY *looks over at* SARAT, *who shrugs her shoulders.*)

SARAT (*moving to* L. *of the stove*).   What does it matter ?

MARY (*calling*).   Come in, Doctor.

(PIERCE *rises warily.* JEFFREYS *enters* L.   *He wears a long white coat, and his stethoscope swings from his hand.*)

JEFFREYS (*as he enters*).   What about that coffee, Sister ?   (*He stops as he sees* SARAT.   *Awkwardly.*)   Oh, I'm sorry—I didn't expect . . .

SARAT.   To see me here ?   Well, now you have, don't be uncomfortable about it.

JEFFREYS.   I would have come to see you at the—at Norwich . . .

SARAT.   Only I told you I didn't want anyone.   Don't worry— there's no ill feeling.   You did your best for me—at the time.

JEFFREYS.   Is there—anything else I can do ?

SARAT (*abruptly*).   Whoever your Church Committee gets to finish off my murals, for God's sake don't let them daub those (*she breaks to the door up* L.C. ; *with a sob*) angels on the left with gold leaf.   It'll ruin everything.

(*She throws down her cigarette and exits abruptly up* L.C.   PIERCE *follows her off.* JEFFREYS *moves to the desk, puts his stethoscope on it, then sits in the chair* L. *of the desk.* MARY *looks at him for a moment, then passes him the folders in which she has been writing.*)

MARY.   This one's up to date.

JEFFREYS.   Thank you.   (*He takes his fountain pen from his breast pocket, unscrews it, then studies the case-papers and makes some notes on them.*)

(MARY *takes another folder and resumes writing.*)

MARY (*after a short pause*).   So you knew her before ?

JEFFREYS. I'm on the Church Committee. When they decided to restore those murals on the South Wall, I recommended Sarat Carn because I'd seen and admired her work.

MARY. It's good, then ?

JEFFREYS. First-rate. She'd a picture in the Academy the year before last.

MARY. What was the subject ?

JEFFREYS. Rather unfortunate in the light of later events. Death of Lucrezia Borgia.

MARY (*slowly*). So it was poison.

JEFFREYS (*shortly*). Yes. It was.

MARY. I don't know the details.

JEFFREYS. Then I shouldn't bother to find out, Sister.

MARY. But . . .

JEFFREYS (*abruptly*). Have you by any chance those slides we made for tests ?

MARY (*rising*). Yes, Doctor. (*She moves to the bookcase, bends down, opens the cupboard and takes out a small tray of microscope slides.*)

(JEFFREYS *continues writing for a moment.* JOSEPHINE *enters* L. *She carries a bright red tray with three cups of steaming coffee.*)

JEFFREYS. And here's Sister Josephine with my coffee. I must say I'm more than ready for it. (*He takes a cup from the tray.*) Thank you, Sister.

(MARY *carries the slides and the microscope from the bookcase and places them on the desk,* R. *of* JEFFREYS, *who sips his coffee meanwhile.*)

JOSEPHINE (*to* MARY). I've brought some for them. Is it all right to take it in ?

MARY. I'm sure they'd appreciate it.

(JOSEPHINE *moves to the door up* L.C.)

JEFFREYS. My word, this is good coffee. What's in it ?

JOSEPHINE (*turning at the door*). If you must know—a soupçon of cognac.

JEFFREYS. Sister Josephine ! (*He puts his cup on the desk.*)

JOSEPHINE. Stimulation, Doctor, stimulation. Very necessary in a time of crisis.

JEFFREYS. I shall personally see this is remembered in your favour at the Day of Judgement.

JOSEPHINE (*with her twinkling smile*). I doubt if we'll arrive there together.

(*She exits with the tray up* L.C.)

MARY (*indicating the microscope*). It's ready, Doctor. (*She passes him a slide.*)

JEFFREYS (*rising and taking the slide*). Thanks.

MARY. So far I know it was poison and the brother was difficult.

JEFFREYS. Difficult! (*Slowly.*) If ever there was a rotten corrupt swine, it was Jason Carn. (*The slide snaps in two in his fingers.*)

(*There is a pause.*)

I beg your pardon, Sister. (*He drops the broken slide into the ashtray.*)
MARY (*gently*). We made a duplicate. (*She takes another slide from the tray and hands it to* JEFFREYS.)
JEFFREYS (*fitting the slide into the microscope*). I told you to forget this business. (*He focusses the eyepiece and looks through the microscope.*) Hullo—hullo. Here we are. Look Sister, this shows the disease was as active as the devil—I beg your pardon—active as anything. (*He eases a little* L., *so that* MARY *can look.*)
MARY (*looking through the microscope*). Then you operated just in time.
JEFFREYS (*sitting* L. *of the desk*). Absolutely. (*He takes another folder, starts to read it, and sips his coffee.*)

(JOSEPHINE *enters up* L.C., *moves to the door* L. *and exits.* MARY *takes the slide out of the microscope and replaces it in the tray.*)

MARY (*taking the slides to the cupboard and putting them away*). Martha seems very concerned about Miss Carn.
JEFFREYS (*putting down his cup, turning and looking at her*). Just why are you so persistent?
MARY (*moving to the desk*). Because I want to know, and you're the one person who can tell me. (*She picks up the microscope.*)
JEFFREYS. And what good can it do if you *do* know?
MARY (*moving to the bookcase*). If I'm ignorant of the facts, I may be tactless with every word I say. (*She places the microscope on the bookcase.*)
JEFFREYS. True enough. (*He shrugs his shoulders.*) Very well. Give me another file while I talk or we'll never get through.

(MARY *moves to the desk, sits in her chair and passes another folder to* JEFFREYS. *They both work while he talks,* MARY *making entries in the black note-books.*)

Where shall I begin?
MARY. At the beginning.
JEFFREYS. Have you ever heard of David Kingham?
MARY. Kingham? Yes—wait a minute—the writer and politician. Isn't he quite a coming man?
JEFFREYS. Not now. He was so prominent in this case and fought for her so desperately, that it's *bound* to have prejudiced his position.
MARY. But why was he dragged into it?
JEFFREYS. He and Sarat were to have been married.
MARY. Oh.
JEFFREYS. He was away on a government mission for six months,

and she wanted to finish the murals in our church before he returned. (*He makes some notes on the case-papers.*) The trouble began when Jason turned up out of the blue and settled at the Grape House. (*He blots a page and turns it.*) I've told you what I thought about Jason.

MARY (*quietly*). Yes.

JEFFREYS. He was a confirmed alcoholic.

MARY. Poor man.

JEFFREYS. Poor ! Sarat had kept him for years. Some weeks after he arrived, he collapsed suddenly, and no wonder.

MARY. A stroke ?

JEFFREYS. Yes. I'd warned him, but he was seldom sober enough to listen. He recovered his mental powers slowly, but he was partially paralysed. Just punishment enough, except that Sarat took the strain.

MARY. Couldn't he have been put in an institution ? (*She takes another notebook and works on it.*)

JEFFREYS. An inebriates' home ? Yes. But these things take time, and one day Sarat called me into the dining-room and asked me frankly just how long he would live. Martha was in the room at the time. She remembers the conversation.

MARY. The tragic thing is that these people drag on for years.

JEFFREYS. Or—as I told her—die quietly in their sleep. She said she was desperate. Her work was suffering and she had written to Kingham postponing her marriage.

MARY. But why do that ?

JEFFREYS. She rightly felt she couldn't saddle him with the responsibility of Jason. Of course, Kingham would have helped her— but she's very proud.

MARY. So I've been told.

JEFFREYS. I promised I would try and arrange an institution, but I warned her such a life might affect Jason's sanity. (*He pauses.*) I remember so well what she said. (*He leans back in his chair, his pen in his hand.*)

MARY (*prompting gently*). Yes ?

JEFFREYS (*slowly*). She said : " While he's well he's on my hands, and while he's ill, he's on my conscience." (*He puts down his pen and takes a cigarette case and matches from his pocket.*)

MARY. Why did you not send him up here to us ?

JEFFREYS. That was hardly fair—he was cut off from his alcohol— all his energy went into an over-active brain and tongue. Nurses just came and went. (*He pauses, match in hand, and looks at the case-papers in front of him.*) Who ordered this luminal for Mrs Thomas ?

MARY. Dr Beauchamp.

JEFFREYS. Oh, right. (*He lights his cigarette, throws the match in the ashtray, picks up his pen and initials the paper. He then passes the folder to* MARY.) Where were we ?

MARY (*passing him another folder*). Sarat is trying to finish a highly-skilled piece of creative work, and arrange her marriage. In the background, a helpless brother is making her days and nights utter misery.

JEFFREYS. That's a pretty comprehensive grasp of the situation, Sister.

MARY. Yes.

JEFFREYS. Except that I was able to ease the nights. We kept him under drugs. It was the only way to bring relief to either of them.

MARY (*looking up from her work*). No night nurse ?

JEFFREYS. Not necessary. The day nurse left at six. At eight, Sarat gave him the drug, one tablet each night. No need for details —it was a narcotic, of course, one of the barbiturates, put up in tablet form. Three weeks' supply was ordered at a time, that is twenty-one tablets, packed singly in a small glass phial.

MARY (*resuming her work*). Where did they come from ?

JEFFREYS. Every three weeks I collected these twenty-one tablets from Abel Harmer, the village chemist. We checked the number into the phial, sealed it and I delivered it to Sarat personally. (*Slowly.*) I warned her not to give more than one tablet in twenty-four hours.

MARY. I—begin to understand.

JEFFREYS. At the end of November, I went to Norwich for three weeks' vacation. I delivered the usual phial the day I left.

MARY. Twenty-one tablets ?

(JEFFREYS *finishes his coffee.*)

JEFFREYS. Yes. Four days later, Dr Giles, my locum, telephoned me to say Jason had been found dead that morning. (*He rises, moves to the stove and drops the stub of his cigarette into it.*) Will it— shock you if I admit my first reaction was one of overwhelming relief ?

MARY. I think I might have felt the same.

JEFFREYS. Until Giles told me that from the evidence of vomiting —and so on—he suspected an overdose of the drug. So he checked the tablets in the phial. (*He moves to L. of* MARY.) Now listen carefully—no, wait—have you got something—here—these will do. (*He empties the box of sweets on to the desk and arranges the sweets to illustrate his meaning as he talks.*) Here it is, Sister. (*He counts out the sweets.*) Ten, twelve—eighteen—twenty-one. (*He puts the re-maining sweets back in the box.*) Twenty-one tablets. One a night for four nights. How many left ?

MARY (*moving aside four sweets*). Four from twenty-one— seventeen.

JEFFREYS (*quietly*). There were seventeen tablets in the phial.

MARY (*glancing at the sweets, then at* JEFFREYS). But I don't see . . .

JEFFREYS. Neither Giles nor I could understand it, either. So I took it on myself to get those seventeen tablets analysed.

MARY. And they found . . . ?

JEFFREYS (*sweeping aside all but two sweets*). Fifteen were correct. The remaining two were harmless aspirin. (*Quietly.*) The police found a half-empty bottle of aspirin in Sarat's room.

MARY (*slowly*). And Jason had had three sleeping tablets that night.

JEFFREYS. Exactly. (*He resumes his seat* L. *of the desk.*) Now do you see why I don't want to be reminded of it all ?

MARY. But couldn't Jason have taken them himself—suicide— and arranged things to look . . . ?

JEFFREYS (*interrupting*). He was paralysed.

MARY (*slowly*). Yes, of course.

JEFFREYS. And as I told you, Martha had been in and out of the room that time Sarat spoke to me. At the inquest they got that damning conversation out of her, practically word for word. (*He sweeps the sweets back into the box and starts to write again.*)

MARY. But this doesn't make sense. Miss Carn's a highly intelligent woman. She would have known you'd suspect an overdose and analyse the phial.

JEFFREYS. Sister, if you had no medical knowledge and gave someone an overdose of a narcotic—how would you expect them to die ?

MARY. I—don't know. I suppose— (*she looks at him*) quietly in their sleep.

JEFFREYS. And *I* told her he *might* die that way.

MARY. Yes, you did. I forgot that.

JEFFREYS. The prosecution didn't, I assure you. In fact the defence wanted her to admit to a mercy killing, but she flatly refused. (*He hands her the folder.*) Is that the lot, Sister ?

MARY. Yes, Doctor.

JEFFREYS (*rising and putting his fountain pen in his pocket*). Right. (*He picks up his stethoscope and moves to the door* L.) I shall be around somewhere if you want me.

(*He exits* L. MARY *pauses a moment, then rises, moves the chair from* L. *of the desk to* L. *of the stove, then moves to the door up* L.C. *and opens it*).

MARY (*speaking off*). Dr Jeffreys has gone now. (*She moves to the desk, stacks the folders, then sits and resumes writing in the notebooks.*)

(SARAT *and* PIERCE *enter up* L.C. SARAT *has discarded her coat.*)

SARAT (*moving* C.). Pierce has an idea she'd like to explore your bookcase. It's a bit dull for her. We played cards at first—but it rather palls.

MARY. Do have whatever you want. Those on the top shelf are mostly textbooks, but there's some fiction lower down.

PIERCE (*moving to the bookcase*). Thank you, Sister. (*She starts to examine the books.*)

(SARAT *moves to the bookcase, stands below* PIERCE *and also examines the books.*)

SARAT.   A better selection than Norwich, eh, Pierce ?

PIERCE.   Yes.

SARAT (*reading the titles*). *Diseases of the Digestive Organs.* Sounds grisly. Biography, *Abraham Lincoln.* Schopenhauer—the intellect is the servant of the will." I wonder ? (*She takes a book from the shelves and opens it.*) Poetry. (*She moves to the window seat, sits, and starts to read.*)

(PIERCE *selects a book, and stands browsing through it by the bookcase.*)

(*She reads aloud.*)   " He was distraught by passion, he spoke in fury, but thou dost judge him with a quiet mind." (*She closes the book, puts it on the window seat, rises and moves to* L. *of the desk. To* MARY.) That's like you, isn't it ? Judge him with a quiet mind. (*Abruptly.*) Have you judged me yet ?

MARY (*looking full at* SARAT ; *quietly*).   Will you tell me something ?   And forgive me for asking ?

SARAT (*with a glint of humour*).   Ar, sure-ley.

MARY.   Why wouldn't you let Counsel plead a mercy killing ?

SARAT.   I'll answer you as I answered him.   Because although I had often wished Jason dead, I had never felt called upon to do anything about it.   Sufficient ?

MARY.   Completely, thank you. (*She resumes writing.*)

SARAT.   Good. (*She starts to pace, with long swinging strides, between the desk and the door* L.)

(PIERCE *glances at* SARAT, *then moves to the window seat, sits, and starts to read.*)

(*After two turns, she pauses. To* MARY.)   Does this worry you ?

MARY.   Not in the least.

SARAT (*pacing to* L.).   That's as well.   I do it a lot.   Pierce is used to it. (*She turns up* L. ; *pauses by the stool and touches the tapestry.*)   This is nice.

MARY.   Yes.   I believe it's very old.

(SARAT *picks up the tapestry, looks at* MARY *and laughs.*)

SARAT.   And you keep it over the big chair in the hall !   To keep out the draught !

MARY (*laughing*).   Well, I had to get your wet coat away somehow.

SARAT.   Masterly strategy. (*She looks critically at the tapestry.*) It doesn't look as if it would keep anything out in its present state. What's wrong—moth ?

MARY.   Age, unfortunately.   We discovered it hidden away, some weeks ago.   Sister Agnes is going to try and repair it, but I'm afraid it's beyond her.

SARAT.   If she's a good needlewoman, I don't see why.

MARY. The design is lost.

SARAT. How do you mean ? (*She drapes the tapestry over the chair* L. *of the stove, and reveals a very large hole almost in the centre.*) I see—the pattern doesn't recur. What a pity. It's magnificently done. Look at the exquisite stitches.

MARY (*rising*). Reverend Mother wanted it restored for the Chapel. But we couldn't do it unless Sister Agnes had something to work from. (*She moves to* R. *of* SARAT. *Slowly.*) What we need is—an artist.

(SARAT *looks up sharply, then shakes her head.*)

SARAT. No, Sister. There isn't time. (*She breaks desperately* L.)

MARY. Would it take so long ?

SARAT (*violently*). No, Sister. (*She moves* L.C.)

MARY (*easing to the tapestry and surveying it*). A piece of plain canvas to back the missing strip, with the design outlined—even roughly . . .

SARAT (*moving down* L.). I'd need materials—colours . . .

MARY. I'm sure we could supply most of them.

SARAT (*turning*). No, Sister—I can't. (*She moves up* L.) Besides, it would have to be on a proper frame.

MARY (*easing* C.). We might even have that. Sister Agnes teaches needlework. (*She pauses.*) And think what we'd have to remember you by.

SARAT (*turning*). Remember me ! (*She moves to* L. *of* MARY.) That would be wonderful. Every time anyone looked at it—and on the Chapel wall of all places—what would they say ? " See that embroidery ? Do you know who designed it ? Sarat Carn—the . . ."

MARY (*quickly*). The artist. Because it might be there for generations. And only the beauty would be remembered.

(SARAT *takes one of her desperate turns up* L., *then moves down to* L. *of* MARY.)

SARAT (*suddenly*). Have you something I can measure with ?

(MARY *moves to the desk, opens a drawer and takes out a steel spring tape measure.* SARAT *picks up the tapestry and spreads it on the floor* C. PIERCE *looks up watchfully.*)

MARY (*offering the tape to* SARAT). Will this do ?

SARAT (*taking the tape*). Thank you. (*She kneels down and measures quickly and deftly.*) We'd have to allow here and there for overlap—say two feet—no, eighteen inches would do. And here again—two feet three. Jot it down, will you, Sister ?

(MARY *moves to the desk, finds a notebook and pencil, and records the measurements.*)

Two feet three long and eighteen inches wide. I shall want fairly coarse canvas—and colours—the primaries and some white— (*she rises*) and gold if you can get it. (*She breaks off.*) But it's quite impossible. (*She puts the tape on the desk.*)

MARY (*joyfully*). It's quite *simple*. All you have to do is rough out your design.

SARAT (*looking at* MARY *and smiling*). What I like about you, Sister, is your supreme disregard of obstacles. All right. Have you a pencil and paper ? (*She moves below the desk and looks on it.*) Here's one. (*She picks up a pencil.*) It wants sharpening. Didn't I see a nice little penknife ? Ah, yes. (*She picks up the penknife from the desk.*)

(PIERCE *rises quickly, moves to* R. *of* SARAT, *catches her wrist in her left hand and takes away the knife.* MARY *takes a sheet of paper from a drawer in the desk.*)

PIERCE (*quietly*). I'll do that, shall I ?

(SARAT'S *face changes. She throws the pencil on to the desk and breaks* C.)

SARAT. If we get that far, Pierce—I might even let you mix the colours.

(JOSEPHINE *enters* L. *and pauses in the doorway.*)

(*She sweeps up the tapestry and drapes it over her arm.*) I know— we'll spread it on the beds—it'll be easier. If you want to help me, Pierce, I'll be grateful. (*She takes the piece of paper from the desk and moves to the door up* L.C. *Over her shoulder.*) You might bring that steel tape, please.

(*She exits up* L.C. PIERCE *picks up the pencil and tape from the desk, crosses to the door up* L.C. *and exits.*)

JOSEPHINE (*looking across at* MARY). I wondered why that tapestry was brought here.

(MARY *studies the list of* SARAT'S *requirements.*)

(*She moves briskly to* L. *of the desk.*) May I have the empties ? We're so short of china and glass we shall soon be drinking out of milk bottles.

(MARY *puts the list on the desk, then fetches the chair from* L. *of the stove and places it* L. *of the desk.*)

MARY. Sit down, Sister Josephine. I need your help. (*She sits at her desk.*)

JOSEPHINE (*sitting* L. *of the desk*). That's a reversion of normal procedure, I must say.

MARY. I've been talking to Miss Carn.

JOSEPHINE. Poor desolate soul.

MARY. Nothing of the kind. She's a brilliant sensitive woman, and from the moment I saw her, something passed between us. It was as if her tragedy—her agony of mind—entered into me.

JOSEPHINE (*gently*). That was only because . . .

MARY. Because I know she is no more guilty of this crime than I am myself.

JOSEPHINE. You can't possibly do anything. Don't, Sister . . .

MARY. I must. It's as if I were—driven from within.

JOSEPHINE. But you're at such a disadvantage.

MARY. I begin with one great advantage. A complete conviction of her innocence.

JOSEPHINE. What could you do against the whole process of the law ?

MARY (*not listening*). I want every possible detail of the trial. Somewhere there's a link—a little flaw. That's why I need you.

JOSEPHINE (*rising*). Me ?

MARY. Those piles of newspapers you're always hoarding—find me every scrap dated January—particularly the local papers.

JOSEPHINE. But I may have used them. It's three weeks gone.

MARY. Go and look, Sister Josephine.

JOSEPHINE. Very well. It's a blessing I'm methodical. (*She crosses to the door* L.) It won't take a second, provided they're there. The cupboard's just outside. But don't break your heart if they're not.

(*She exits* L. MARY *lifts the telephone receiver and dials.*)

MARY (*into the telephone*). Sister Agnes, could we lay hands on some of the old school materials ? . . . No—poster paints for preference . . . Oh, good . . . Yes, urgently. Miss Carn is going to do the design for your tapestry . . . Yes—I've a list—I knew you'd help . . . That would be wonderful. And have we a tapestry frame ? . . . Well, Willy can mend it—he's an excellent carpenter . . . Thank you, Sister. (*She replaces the receiver.*)

(JOSEPHINE *enters* L. *She carries two bundles of newspapers.*)

JOSEPHINE (*moving* C.). There's organization for you. Here— you take the London ones and I'll take the locals. (*She puts the papers on the floor and kneels above one pile.*)

(MARY *moves to* R. *of her, kneels above the second pile and checks through it.*)

(*She checks through the pile.*) December, December, January—here we are. First, seventh— (*she opens a paper*) no—nothing there.

MARY. January fourteenth. (*She extracts a paper from her pile.*) This is it. (*She opens out the paper.*)

(JOSEPHINE *leans over to look.*)

(*She reads slowly.*) " The case against Sarat Carn."

JOSEPHINE (*reading*). " Trial of noted artist opens at Assizes."

MARY. There's her Academy picture—Jeffreys told me—my
word, look at the power of that drawing. (*Suddenly*.) What are we
waiting for—where's January twenty-first ?

JOSEPHINE (*selecting a paper from her pile*). Here's more pictures
and nearly a page—the summing up.

MARY (*taking the paper from her*). That's what I want. (*She
reads*.) " Result of Fen case." (*Slowly*.) " Sarat Carn to h . . . "
(*She puts the paper down*.) Where's the local paper for January
twenty-first ? We must have that—it's bound to be practically
verbatim.

(*They search feverishly through their piles*.)

JOSEPHINE. Not here, I'm afraid.

MARY. It must be. It has to be. (*She leans over and searches
through* JOSEPHINE'S *pile*.) Why should that particular issue be lost
or destroyed ? Think, Sister Josephine, think !

JOSEPHINE. January—what happened here in January ? I did all
the cupboards—the linen cupboards—for the New Year. No—I
used *The Times* for those.

MARY. Then we must look through every cupboard . . .

JOSEPHINE. It would take a day.

MARY. But . . .

JOSEPHINE. Wait now—don't rush me. Let me go through it in
my mind.

MARY. It . . .

JOSEPHINE. No, don't say anything for a moment. (*She sits back
on her heels and ticks the items off on her fingers*.) I did the linen—
the nurses' rooms—no, that was in December. The storeroom—
no, no papers, we scrub the shelves. (*She pauses*.) We did your
cupboard—(*she points to the cupboard under the bookcase*) that
one there.

(*They look at each other, then rise and move to the cupboard. MARY's
hands tremble as she opens the cupboard*.)

Let me. (*She looks at the papers lining the shelves*.) It's a local
right enough—though I don't remember using it here. December—
October previous and December—no, not here.

MARY (*moving to L. of the desk*). Then we must think again.

JOSEPHINE (*still peering into the cupboard*). Och—this is a wild-
goose chase. And this could do wi' another turn-out sometime.
Why does Dr Jeffreys keep all this old microscope stuff ? If he'd
throw it out I could have the boxes.

(MARY *kneels and looks again through the papers on the floor* c.)

(*She reaches into the cupboard and extracts a parcel wrapped in newspaper*.) What's this ? (*She carries the parcel to the desk and looks at
it. Suddenly*.) Sister Mary !

MARY (*looking up*). What is it ?

JOSEPHINE (*beaming*). January the twenty-first.

(MARY *rises, moves above the desk, takes the parcel from* JOSEPHINE, *looks at it, then at* JOSEPHINE.)

MARY. Sister Josephine—what *should* I do without you ?—bless your busy heart.

(*The telephone rings.*)

(*She gives the parcel to* JOSEPHINE.) Unwrap it, quickly ! (*She lifts the receiver.*)

(JOSEPHINE, R. *of the desk, slips the string off the parcel, rolls the string up neatly and puts it in her pocket.*)

(*Into the telephone.*) Sister Bonaventure . . . Yes ? . . . Yes, Sister Agnes. Keep him with you. I want to talk to him about the carpentry. Sister Josephine is bringing you down the list . . . Yes. Right away. (*She replaces the receiver and hands the list to* JOSEPHINE.) For Sister Agnes.

(JOSEPHINE *takes the list and crosses below the desk to the door* L.)

JOSEPHINE (*reading as she goes*). The primaries—and some white. And gold if we can get it.

(*She exits* L.)

MARY (*looking up and smiling*). We'll get it. (*She picks up the newspaper wrapping and reads it.*)

CURTAIN

SCENE 2

SCENE.—*The same. Early the next evening.*
    A large tapestry frame now stands L.C. *The piece of tapestry is spread over it. The hole is now filled in and the new canvas shows a bold scene partly filled with rich colour. There is a stool above the frame. Another* R. *of the frame has on it a tray of paints, a piece of rag, a palette, some paint brushes in a jam jar and one or two pencils. A toolbag and a hammer are on the chair* L. *of the desk.*
When the CURTAIN *rises, the lights are lit and a bright fire burns in the stove.* SARAT *is seated on the stool above the frame.* MELLING *stands looking over* SARAT'S *left shoulder.* WILLY, *with a hammer in his hand, stands* R. *of the frame.* MARY *is seated at her desk, writing.* PIERCE *enters up* L.C. *and stands* L. *of the stove.*

SARAT (*brightly ; to* WILLY). It's a bit loose in this corner. Pass me the hammer, will you, Willy ? (*She reaches out for the hammer.*)
    MELLING (*quietly intercepting and taking the hammer from* WILLY). I'll do that, shall I ?

(SARAT *rises abruptly and breaks to* L.)

(*He returns the hammer to* WILLY *and moves to* SARAT.   *Quietly.*)
I'm sorry.

SARAT (*savagely, almost under her breath*).   Damn you—damn you
—why can't you let me forget for a moment ?

MELLING.   It's our training, I suppose.

WILLY (R. *of the frame ; looking at the tapestry*).   It's that bright
and grand, Miss Sarat.   Look at this lovely lady in the purple dress
—and who's this fellow wi' the long nose in yellow botes ?

SARAT (*crossing below* MELLING *to the frame*).   He's flirting with
the lovely lady, riding rather close and looking into her eyes.

WILLY.   If he dassn't look at his horse now and again, he's going
the right way to fall off into the muck.

PIERCE (*moving between* WILLY *and* SARAT).   Willy, we're very
grateful for the frame.   Will you take your tools now, and fix up
that bunting downstairs ?   (*She moves to the chair* R. *of the stove
and sits.*)

WILLY.   Yes, miss.   (*He picks up the toolbag, puts the hammer in
it and moves to* L. *of* SARAT.)   There's going to be a party in the Big
Hall tonight, Miss Sarat.   Reverend Mother said so—for us and the
refugees.   Will 'e give me a dance like that time in the Church Hall
when you were doin' them big pictures ?

SARAT (*sitting at the frame*).   I'm sorry, but I won't be coming.
(*She selects a paint brush and starts to paint.*)

WILLY.   Not coming ?   Why—Ted Newlands is fixin' the wire-
less gramophone for *real* music.

MELLING (*clapping* WILLY *on the shoulder*).   That's enough, boy.
You go along and help Newlands.

(WILLY *shakes* MELLING'S *hand off and continues to speak to* SARAT.)

WILLY.   Right smart wi' his hands, that Ted is, Miss Sarat.   He
were saying he might even get the telephone wires mended soon—
maybe tomorrow.

(PIERCE *rises.*)

SARAT (*turning to* WILLY ; *involuntarily*).   Telephone !

MELLING (*firmly*).   Downstairs, Willy.   (*He moves to the door* L.
and opens it.)   And jump to it.

WILLY (*turning to* MELLING *and raising his voice in sudden anger*).
All right, then, since you be so sharp . . .

MARY (*looking up*).   Willy——

(WILLY *stands still, his back to* MARY.)

WILLY.   Yes, Sister ?

MARY (*smiling*).   —will you take a message to Sister Josephine
for me ?   Listen carefully now.   Say I would like one of her special
caramel custards—the ones with cream on top—for Mrs Grimes.
Can you remember ?

WILLY (*slowly*).   Cara-mel custards—wi' cream on top.   (*He turns to* MARY *and his face breaks into a smile.*)   Ar, sure-ley.   I know. Praper tasty, they be.

MARY.   Thank you, Willy.   You're very helpful.   (*She resumes writing.*)

(*Quite happy, and with a smile,* WILLY *exits* L. *with his toolbag.* MELLING *closes the door.* PIERCE *resumes her seat.*)

MELLING (*moving above* SARAT).   I'm sorry.   I'll tell him he's not to come up here again.

SARAT (*putting down her paint brush and picking up a pencil*).   And he's the one person who's at ease with me.   (*Abruptly.*)   You might sharpen that, would you, please ?   (*She passes him the pencil over her left shoulder, then picks up her paint brush and resumes painting.*)

(MELLING *takes a clasp knife from his pocket, moves to the stove, and sharpens the pencil.*)

What's this about the telephone ?

MELLING.   Just talk, I shouldn't wonder.

SARAT.   If by the grace of God, and the genius of Ted Newlands, it *is* fixed, I suppose—you'll get through to the Governor.

MELLING (*moving to* R. *of* SARAT).   Miss Carn, you do realize this situation must end soon ?

SARAT (*abruptly*).   Yes, I realize.   By the way, not too fine a point for this canvas, please.

MELLING (*holding out the pencil*).   This do ?

SARAT (*taking the pencil*).   Admirably, thank you very much. (*She puts the pencil on the stool and resumes painting.*)

(MELLING *returns his knife to his pocket, then moves* L. *of* SARAT *and looks at the tapestry.*)

MELLING.   It certainly does grow.

SARAT.   I find things do—when one is pressed for time.

MELLING (*glancing at his wrist-watch*).   Not so pressed you can't take a little exercise.

SARAT.   Thanks.   I've had all the exercise I want for one day.

(*There is a tap at the door* L., *and* JEFFREYS *enters.*)

JEFFREYS.   Oh, I beg your pardon—I thought . . .

MELLING.   Can you give us two minutes, sir ?   We're just going for a stroll.

JEFFREYS.   Certainly.

(*He turns and exits* L.)

MELLING.   You've been working solidly, Miss Carn, and I expect the doctor wants to talk to Sister, so it's all nice and convenient. We might go up to the top of the tower again and have a look at the floods before it gets dark.   (*He looks over at* PIERCE *and nods.*)

(PIERCE *rises and moves to* R. *of* SARAT.)

SARAT.   I wonder you're not afraid I'll jump off.

MELLING.   I'll have to risk that, won't I ?

(SARAT *stops painting, and, brush in hand, looks from* MELLING *to*
PIERCE, *closed in, one each side of her. Suddenly, she throws the
brush down on to the stool and rises.*)

SARAT.   Officer, I know you and Miss Pierce have to hand me
over in good condition, but so long as I can stand on my feet when—
the time comes—can't you let me do something worthwhile when
I've got the chance ?

MELLING.   You'll work all the fresher for a bit of a blow, don't
you think ?

SARAT (*turning to* MARY ; *desperately*).   Sister . . .

(MELLING *picks up* SARAT'S *coat from the stool up* L. *and puts the coat
over* SARAT'S *shoulders.*)

MELLING (*firmly*).   Come along now, Miss Carn.

SARAT.   I should say your tenacity will make you a Governor
early in life.

MELLING (*opening the door* L.).   My ambitions don't lie that way.
My hobby is Siamese cats.

(SARAT *and* PIERCE *exit* L.   MELLING *follows them off.*)

(*Off. To* JEFFREYS.)   We'll be about fifteen minutes, sir.

JEFFREYS (*off*).   Thank you, Officer.

(JEFFREYS *enters* L.   *He carries a small bag.*)

(*He moves to the desk and puts the bag on the chair* L. *of it.*)   Sister,
can you let me have a length of gauze ?   It's only for my bag.

MARY (*rising*).   Certainly, Doctor.   (*She moves to the bookcase
cupboard and opens it.*)

JEFFREYS.   They're short of it in surgery.   (*He stands by the desk,
sees the newspaper cuttings in their clip, picks them up and glances
through them. He glances at* MARY, *then at the cuttings again.*)

(MARTHA *enters* L.   *She carries a bucket of logs.*   MARY *takes a roll
of surgical gauze from the cupboard.*)

MARTHA.   I beg your pardon, Sister.

MARY (*turning*).   Yes, Martha—what is it ?

(JEFFREYS *replaces the cuttings on the desk.*)

MARTHA (*moving to* L. *of the stove*).   I brought the logs up—
Willy's busy cleanin' 'imself for the party.   And please, could you
fix one of the men ?   'E's jagged himself praper nasty nailin' up the
flags.

MARY (*moving above the desk*).   Very well, Martha, I'll see to it.

(MARTHA *places the bucket* L. *of the stove, then moves to the door* L.)

JEFFREYS (*rather sharply*). Send him up to surgery, Martha, and I'll see to it. Sister's very busy and it's time people stopped running to her over trifles.

MARTHA. Ar, but seein' as tes all free 'ere, they're quick to take advantage. Like as not if they were down 'ome they'd clap on 'andful o' cobwebs and think no more about it.

JEFFREYS. At a later stage, Martha, we'd do precisely the same thing. Only we'd call it penicillin.

MARTHA. Indeed, sir ? It only goes to show 'ow backward is progress.

(*She exits* L. MARY *unrolls the gauze on the desk.* JEFFREYS *moves to the tapestry and looks at it.*)

MARY. Take as much as you like while it's here. (*She pauses and looks across to him. Quietly.*) What a feeling she has for colour !

JEFFREYS. Yes. Let's hope this doesn't remain like the murals—unfinished.

MARY. I've a feeling they may both be finished.

JEFFREYS (*looking up*). Oh ? (*He moves suddenly to* L. *of her.*) Sister, surely you're not still trying to convince yourself . . .

MARY (*taking a pair of scissors from the desk drawer*). Perhaps something is trying to convince me. (*She spreads out the gauze.*) How much do you want ? (*She indicates with the scissors.*) To here ?

JEFFREYS. A little more if you can spare it—yes, like that. Thank you.

MARY (*cutting off a length of gauze*). You think I'm still taking too personal an interest ?

JEFFREYS. I do think it's a pity to cause yourself so much mental distress.

MARY. What causes me real distress of mind is the way everyone is accepting the situation. (*She rewinds the roll of gauze.*)

JEFFREYS. Sister, has it occurred to you that instead of developing these—these fantastic ideas, you might be of some practical use ?

MARY. If only I could. (*She tucks the roll under her arm and starts to fold the cut-off piece.*)

JEFFREYS (*moving below the* L. *end of the desk and standing with his back to the audience*). I'll do that while you put the roll away.

(MARY *turns, moves to the bookcase and replaces the roll of gauze in the cupboard.*)

(*He lifts his bag on to the* L. *end of the desk with his right hand, and with his back to the audience, folds the gauze, opens the bag, puts the gauze in it, then shuts it, picks it up and moves* C.) I suppose Sarat hasn't mentioned David Kingham to you ?

MARY. No.

JEFFREYS. Since the—verdict, she's refused to see him or even write.

MARY (*moving to the desk*). Why ? (*She sits at the desk.*)

JEFFREYS. She maintains she's ruined things for him, socially, politically, and in every way.

MARY. I can understand how she feels, especially if she loves him.

JEFFREYS (*moving to* L. *of the desk*). It's ridiculous—stubborn to the point of madness. (*Earnestly.*) Sister, Sarat will listen to you. Will you try and persuade her to see him before—or even write a note ? Her attitude is causing them both unnecessary suffering.

MARY. It's a very delicate and personal matter. I can't promise. You must leave it to me.

JEFFREYS. Gladly. But do your best, for God's sake. (*He moves to the door* L.)

MARY. You feel very deeply about this case, don't you ?

JEFFREYS (*turning and easing* C.). If only I hadn't taken that dam' vacation in Norwich—if only I'd been on the spot instead of Giles.

(*The telephone rings.* MARY *lifts the receiver.*)

MARY (*into the telephone*). Sister Bonaventure . . . Yes, he's here. One moment. (*She holds out the receiver to* JEFFREYS.) Doctor—it's for you.

(JEFFREYS *moves to the desk and takes the receiver.*)

JEFFREYS (*into the telephone*). Hullo . . . Yes, speaking . . . All right. I'll come. (*He replaces the receiver.*) They want me to look at the Grimes' baby.

(MARY *rises.*)

No, no—I'll ring down if I need you. (*He moves to the door* L.)

MARY (*resuming her seat*). Doctor—if you hadn't been in Norwich when Jason died—would there have been a post-mortem ?

JEFFREYS. No. (*Abruptly.*) I would have signed a death certificate in any circumstances.

(*He exits quickly* L., *almost colliding with* JOSEPHINE, *who enters* L. *at that moment.*)

(*As he goes.*) Sorry, Sister.

(JOSEPHINE *looks after him in surprise, then closes the door.*)

JOSEPHINE (*moving* C.). Hmph ! He's energetic tonight.

MARY. Yes. He's been called up to the Grimes' baby. Isn't it lovely it should be a little son ?

JOSEPHINE (*drily*). No doubt, after five girls. And I'm here about that business myself. Just how do you expect me to produce delicacies on the dot—without cream, with practically no eggs, and the milk getting to the stage when we shall have to water it ? Because . . .

MARY (*smiling*). Because I know you can work miracles at a moment's notice.

JOSEPHINE. Miracles, yes. But you want the impossible. And that takes a wee while longer.

(MARY *picks up the cuttings and looks at them.*)

(*Gently.*) As I've no doubt you're finding out for yourself.

MARY. The evidence is so damning, it frightens me. (*She looks up.*) How *did* Jason take those two extra tablets ?

JOSEPHINE. Could they not have been put in his food ?

MARY. No. That was established from the first. Sarat has never denied giving him the usual dose at eight o'clock. Remember —he couldn't have reached the phial himself. And Sarat was alone with him all that night.

JOSEPHINE. Aye.

MARY. Listen. (*She refers to the cuttings.*) This is Counsel for the Defence. (*She reads.*) " Members of the jury, you are asked by the Prosecution to accept the fact that this woman deliberately and with malice aforethought administered an overdose of tablets. Yet, having laid careful plans, the accused neglects the simple—I might say elementary—precaution of acquainting herself with the symptoms of such an overdose. You are asked to believe this extra-ordinary oversight on the part of an extraordinarily intelligent woman. I submit to you that the idea is preposterous."

JOSEPHINE. That's a man of sense.

MARY (*referring to another cutting*). And this is the Prosecution. (*She reads.*) " My learned friend has pointed out what he calls an extraordinary oversight on the part of an intelligent woman. But he has previously admitted the prisoner to be of a passionate and artistic temperament. Be that as it may, these are things of emotion. The Prosecution is concerned with plain facts, and the plain facts are these. Sarat Carn had every reason to desire her brother's death. She had the means to hand ; and from the time the undoubtedly fatal dose was administered, at eight o'clock, no-one visited the house until the arrival of Martha Pentridge next morning." (*She looks up. Quietly.*) Another man of sense, Sister.

JOSEPHINE. And you think you're going to beat them both.

MARY (*putting the cuttings on the desk*). The impossible takes a wee while longer.

JOSEPHINE. Sister—what's it going to do to you if you fail ?

MARY. I daren't fail. (*She rises.*) Never in my whole religious life have I needed a sign from heaven more desperately than I do now. (*Earnestly.*) I *daren't* fail. And I can't waste precious time —Night Sister is waiting for her reports. (*She puts the cuttings in the desk drawer and picks up the four black notebooks.*)

(SARAT, MELLING *and* PIERCE *enter* L. SARAT *looks flushed with exercise and her hair is blown about.*)

SARAT (*slipping her coat off her shoulders*). Hullo, Sister Josephine. My word, there's a gale up on that tower. (*She crosses to the chair* L. *of the desk and puts her coat on it.*) I didn't realize we were such a height. (*She moves below the desk to the window.*)

(PIERCE *moves to* R. *of the stove,* MELLING *to* L. *of it.*)

JOSEPHINE. I've not been up there for years. What's the view like these days ?

SARAT (*looking out of the window*). A waste of waters. Nothing else for miles. It looks very desolate—and yet it's beautiful. (*She sits on the window seat.*)

MELLING. Worst floods in living memory, I should think.

JOSEPHINE. So *they* say. (*Briskly.*) Well, I can't stand here blethering, with some kind of meal to conjure out of thin air. (*She crosses to the door* L. *and turns. To* MARY.) I should think your precious custard is cool by now. But you're to take it up yourself. Where my cooking is concerned, I don't trust your nurses an inch.

MARY (*crossing to the door ; laughing*). I don't blame them in the least, and you ought to be very proud of it.

(JOSEPHINE *opens the door for her, and* MARY *exits* L. *The sound of dance music is heard off.*)

JOSEPHINE. Pride is a most deadly sin, and to be avoided at all costs. There must be many cooks as good as me within fifty miles. (*She pauses and gives her twinkling smile.*) But I'd like fine to meet them.

(*She exits* L. PIERCE *sits on the chair* R. *of the stove.*)

MELLING (*glancing at his watch*). I'll go down to tea, now.

PIERCE. Right.

MELLING. Then you might like to go off till ten-thirty. Why not look in at the party ?

PIERCE. I might.

MELLING. Newlands'll be there. Do you good.

PIERCE. Isn't their organization incredible ? Masses of people packed in, supplies stacked everywhere, the hospital full, and yet they arrange a party and allow the nurses to join in.

MELLING. It's the woman behind it all I find so incredible. (*He moves to the door* L.)

PIERCE. Shout when you come back.

(MELLING *exits* L. SARAT *rises, moves to the tapestry, looks at it for a few moments, then raises her head and stands listening to the dance music, a gay waltz, heard in the distance.*)

SARAT (*suddenly*). Pierce, I'd like a wash.

(*She turns and exits abruptly up* L.C.)

PIERCE (*rising*). Yes, Miss Carn.

(*She exits up* L.C. *There is a pause. The music is heard more distinctly, then* PHILLIPS *and* BRENT *enter hurriedly* L.)

PHILLIPS (*as she enters*). In here.

BRENT (*breathlessly*). Flippers—you shouldn't—we oughtn't to be here.

PHILLIPS. We've got to give Willy the slip.

BRENT. But you attract him by being so horrible. You know—how a cat will always jump on the one person who doesn't like it.

PHILLIPS (*moving to the stove and warming her hands*). He'll forget about us in a minute, and then we'll go down again.

BRENT. But this is Sister Mary's room. (*She moves down* L.)

PHILLIPS. That doesn't make it sacred. (*She looks around.*) It's certainly comfortable. I thought they had to forswear physical ease.

(*She stops suddenly as* SARAT, *followed by* PIERCE, *enters up* L.C.
BRENT *gasps.* SARAT *pauses for an instant, then crosses to the chair*
L. *of the desk.*)

SARAT (*quietly*). Good evening. (*She picks up her coat, turns and moves to the door up* L.C. *Pleasantly.*) I hope you're having a nice party.

(*With her head held high, she exits up* L.C. PIERCE *follows her off.*)

BRENT (*breathlessly*). That's *her !* Willy wasn't lying—Flippers —it's her.

PHILLIPS. Well, of all the brazen . . .

BRENT. I'm frightened. L-let's go b-back.

(WILLY *enters suddenly* L., *closes the door and puts his back against it.
He wears an ill-fitting dark jacket, a wide bright tie and a fresh shirt.
His hair is slicked back.*)

WILLY. So there you be.

PHILLIPS. Open that door at once. And stop following me everywhere.

BRENT (*easing to* WILLY *and laying her hand tentatively on his arm*).
Willy . . .

(*Without looking at* BRENT, WILLY *thrusts her off. She falls back
against the wall down* L.)

WILLY (*to* PHILLIPS). Why do yee hate me so much ?

PHILLIPS (*impatiently*). I don't hate you.

WILLY. But you do. Every time I so much as speak, every time you pass me—I know you do. And Sister Mary—she says it's wrong to hate people.

PHILLIPS. Sister Mary ! I might have known. (*She moves* C.
Firmly.) Open that door at once.

(WILLY *moves* C. *to meet* PHILLIPS, *who forthwith backs slowly away above the desk.* BRENT *sees the way is clear, opens the door* L. *and exits hurriedly.*)

WILLY (*following* PHILLIPS). See ? You're moving away from me now. I only want to be friends, honest.

(PHILLIPS *moves to* R. *of the desk.*)

(*He moves to* L. *of the desk.*) I wouldn't hurt'ee—I wouldn't hurt anyone. (*He stops* L. *of the desk.*)

PHILLIPS (*speaking across the desk*). All right. That's settled. (*She edges cautiously down* R., *then makes a sudden run towards the door* L.)

(WILLY *catches her* C. *He holds her tightly without any effort, as she struggles.*)

WILLY (*muddled*). It's in the book Sister reads. Somethin' about —if thy neighbour hate thee . . .

PHILLIPS (*struggling furiously*). But I don't hate you. You can't get the simplest thing right.

WILLY. There aren't no need to be frightened. I'm strong right enough, but I'm gentle. Real gentle.

PHILLIPS (*panicking*). Stop it, stop it—do you hear ?

WILLY. Don't 'ee struggle now. (*He holds her firmly but gently, pulls her close to him and kisses her full on the mouth.*)

(PHILLIPS *screams.*)

PHILLIPS. You half-witted beast !

(MELLING *and* MARY *rush in* L., *with* BRENT *close behind them.* MELLING *catches* WILLY *by the shoulders and pulls him* L.)

MARY. Willy !

MELLING. Steady there, lad.

(PHILLIPS *falls back against the desk.*)

(*To* WILLY.) Better go downstairs.

WILLY (*bewildered*). But Sister—I didn't mean no harm.

MARY. I know, Willy. I'll see to it. You go down with Nurse Brent.

BRENT. Come on, Willy. (*She takes his arm sympathetically.*)

WILLY (*suddenly frightened ; to* MARY, *protestingly*). But it were like you said—I wanted to be friends.

MARY. Yes. All right. Run along, now.

WILLY (*almost in tears*). I only wanted to be friends.

(*Still protesting, he exits* L. *with* BRENT. MELLING *closes the door.*)

MARY (*easing down* L.C.). I'm very sorry, Nurse Phillips. You're not hurt, are you ?

(JOSEPHINE *enters* L.)

PHILLIPS (*moving* C. ; *angrily*).   My God—he's no right to be here.   He'll injure someone and when he does it'll be your fault——

(SARAT, *followed by* PIERCE, *enters up* L.C.)

—filling the place with morons—and allowing that woman there . . .

(SARAT *makes an involuntary movement*.   PIERCE *restrains her*.)

(*She shouts*.)   You've no right—no damn right . . .

MARY (*crisply*).   Nurse, either lower your voice or leave this room.

PHILLIPS (*wildly*).   I *will* shout if I please—you trade on your habit, standing there so calm and saintly—you're nothing but . . .

(SARAT *makes one wild rush, so quickly that for the moment,* MELLING *and* PIERCE *are taken off their guard*.   SARAT *seizes* PHILLIPS *and sends her spinning to crash on the floor below the desk*.)

SARAT (*blazing with rage ; hoarsely*).   You little fiend—how dare you !

(*Before she has finished speaking,* MELLING *and* PIERCE, *neatly and efficiently, with a minimum of movement, close on her and pinion her arms behind her back*.)

MELLING.   Now, Miss Carn—if you please.

(*With the same smooth efficiency,* MELLING *and* PIERCE *lead* SARAT *off up* L.C.)

SARAT (*as she goes*).   How dare you—how dare you !

(MARY *moves quietly to* PHILLIPS *and bends down to help her*.   PHILLIPS *thrusts her off savagely*.   MARY *straightens up*.)

MARY (*easing* L. *of the desk ; quietly*).   Now please go up to your room and wait there till I come.

PHILLIPS.   I'll do nothing of the sort.   I'll . . .

MARY (*crisply*).   You are under my authority, Nurse.   You will do exactly as I say .

PHILLIPS (*rising*).   Very well.   (*She moves to the door* L., *then turns, suddenly furious again*.)   But first I'm going to see the Reverend Mother.   It's time she knew about you and your fine ideas.

(*She turns and exits quickly* L., *leaving the door open, and is heard hammering on a door and calling*.)

(*Off.   Calling*.)   Reverend Mother, Reverend Mother.   May I come in ?

(MARY *moves above the desk*.   JOSEPHINE *shuts the door, then moves to the chair* L. *of the desk and sits limply*.)

MARY.   She's quite right.   This *is* my fault.   (*She pauses*.) Why, Sister, you're shaken.

JOSEPHINE.   Her face—did you see Sarat's face.

MARY.   Why ?

JOSEPHINE. Are you sure you're right ?
MARY (*firmly*). Yes. Quite sure.
JOSEPHINE (*simply*). I wish I felt the same.

(SARAT, MELLING *and* PIERCE *enter up* L.C. *This time there is no pretence. They have* SARAT *between them, each with a restraining hand on her arm. They move down* L.C.)

SARAT. I want to say I'm sorry—so very sorry.
MARY (*moving to* R. *of the group*). You mustn't blame Nurse Phillips. She was badly frightened. I'm used to Willy and I forget other people are not.
SARAT. But to speak to you like that . . .
MARY. Don't distress yourself. (*Gently*.) Perhaps you would like to try and rest until after supper, and then go on with your work.
SARAT (*in a very low voice*). Yes, Sister Mary.

(MELLING *and* PIERCE *lead* SARAT *to the door up* L.C., *and all three exit.* MARY *crosses to* L., *then with an involuntary gesture, she turns to the door up* L.C. *As she does so,* MELLING *enters up* L.C.)

MARY. Poor unhappy child . . .
MELLING. Not now, Sister, if you don't mind.
MARY. But I must speak to Miss Carn.
MELLING. She's not coming out again tonight, Sister. She must be made to understand she can't behave like this.
MARY (*looking at him ; appalled*). You must let me go to her.
MELLING. No, Sister, I'm sorry. Sympathy is all very well, but you must *not* lose sight of her position.
MARY (*after a pause ; deliberately*). Officer, this part of the Convent is in my charge.
MELLING (*quietly but firmly*). Yes, Sister, and Miss Carn is in mine.

(*They measure glances. As they do so, the* MOTHER SUPERIOR *enters* L. JOSEPHINE *rises*.)

MOTHER SUPERIOR (*easing down* L.). Will you excuse me, Officer ?
MELLING. With pleasure, madam.

(*He turns and exits up* L.C. MARY *moves above the desk*.)

MOTHER SUPERIOR. Sister Josephine, I'm sure you must have some work to do.
JOSEPHINE (*unhappily*). I'll go and get their supper.

(*She moves to the door* L. *and exits*.)

MOTHER SUPERIOR (*moving* C.). I have just heard a very hurried and almost incredible account of events here. I should like to ask if it is correct.
MARY. I have never found Nurse Phillips untruthful.

MOTHER SUPERIOR. She has been sent to her room. Until she leaves, it might be advisable to give her only light duties. And perhaps Willy should not be allowed so much freedom. For a little while at any rate.

MARY. I feel that is a pity.

MOTHER SUPERIOR. So do I, Sister. But this is a dreadful thing altogether, and is going to reflect on all of us. (*She pauses.*) I now have to speak against my personal inclinations. (*She moves to the chair* L. *of the desk and sits.*) I want you to understand and bear with me.

MARY (*easing* R. *of the desk*). Yes, Reverend Mother.

MOTHER SUPERIOR. I have always known you held certain strong contentions about Miss Carn. Your views do credit to your sympathy and imagination, and I wouldn't for a second decry them. But there are times when all the compassion in the world is powerless.

MARY. To succeed, but not to stop trying.

MOTHER SUPERIOR (*gently*). A somewhat negative statement, surely? And I—think you have tried enough. (*She pauses and folds her hands in her lap.*) Sister, you asked me to let you be in contact with Miss Carn. Against my better judgement I allowed it. But you were asked by myself and the warders not to raise unreasonable hopes.

MARY. I assure you I've not mentioned anything to *her*.

MOTHER SUPERIOR. You've raised your own hopes and allowed yourself to be carried away by personal emotions. Isn't that true?

MARY. I suppose it is.

MOTHER SUPERIOR. Hasn't it occurred to you that matters reach a stage when they are in other—and greater—hands than ours?

MARY (*quietly, but tensely*). Reverend Mother, can you possibly reconcile the fact that any God—of any creed——

MOTHER SUPERIOR (*raising her hand*). Please . . .

MARY. —I repeat—of any creed—could permit such a cruel and terrible matter as this?

MOTHER SUPERIOR. Everything possible has been done in scrupulous fairness.

MARY. I cannot agree.

MOTHER SUPERIOR. So you place yourself above the highest legal wisdom?

MARY. Which is secular in approach and reasoning.

MOTHER SUPERIOR (*gently*). I see. You feel you are in some manner—blessed—in your reasoning?

MARY (*quietly*). I wouldn't presume so far as that. (*Earnestly.*) I only know that never in my whole life have I been filled with such strong—such complete conviction.

MOTHER SUPERIOR. Then you must destroy it.

MARY. How?

MOTHER SUPERIOR. I can only suggest by faith and prayer. Remember—the whole foundation of our training is to accept.

MARY. Blindly?

MOTHER SUPERIOR. We enter into this life to do the work of God. We learn to subdue our bodies by labour, and submit our wills to higher direction.

MARY. I cannot think we should also subdue our intelligence.

MOTHER SUPERIOR. Even intelligence cannot always recognize Divine intention.

MARY (*suddenly*). I will *not* believe this is Divine intention. (*Slowly.*) If it should be—then I have no use for such a doctrine.

(*The* MOTHER SUPERIOR *rises and faces* MARY *across the desk.*)

MOTHER SUPERIOR. Sister Mary! You cannot make that kind of bargain.

(MARY *turns to the window and stands looking out.*)

(*She moves the chair from* L. *of the desk to* L. *of the stove, then moves above the* L. *end of the desk and holds out her hand.*) Let me see those records of the trial.

MARY (*turning and moving above the* R. *end of the desk*). So she even told you that.

MOTHER SUPERIOR. I know about them.

(MARY *takes the cuttings out of the desk drawer and unclips them.*)

Why are you so proud and so obstinate? You are privileged to handle many lives, but you are not permitted to pass judgement.

MARY (*holding out the cuttings*). So you think Miss Carn—was responsible?

MOTHER SUPERIOR (*taking the cuttings*). I think there is nothing we can do to save Miss Carn, but I know I must try to save you from yourself. (*She moves to* L. *of the stove, opens the lid, then holds the cuttings out to* MARY.)

MARY (*involuntarily*). Oh, no! It's her *life*. Reverend Mother —her *life* may be there.

MOTHER SUPERIOR. It is the best way, Sister.

MARY. Please—I beg of you—don't ask me . . .

MOTHER SUPERIOR. As your personal superior, I order you.

(MARY *clasps her hands and breaks up* R. *Then she turns, faces the* MOTHER SUPERIOR, *and takes a step towards her.*)

MARY (*stopping*). I—can't.

MOTHER SUPERIOR. We have heard a great deal about discipline, Sister, but ours is a discipline of the spirit. (*She drops the cuttings into the stove and closes it.*)

(*The glow of the fire increases for a few moments.*)

(*She moves to the door* L. *Quietly.*) Try to—forgive me.

She exits L. MARY *stands very still by the flickering stove as—*

the CURTAIN *falls.*

ACT III

SCENE 1

SCENE.—*The same. Next afternoon.*

When the CURTAIN *rises,* SARAT *is standing below the tapestry frame looking through the pages of a book.* PIERCE *is seated on the window seat looking through a book, and* MELLING *is similarly occupied, standing in front of the stove. More books are piled on the desk. The chair from* L. *of the stove is standing* L. *of the desk. Daylight comes through the windows, the lights have not been lit and a bright fire burns in the stove.*

PIERCE (*rising and moving above the desk*). Is this any use ? (*She indicates something in her book.*)

(SARAT *puts her book on the stool* R. *of the frame and moves above the desk.*)

SARAT (*taking the book from* PIERCE). Let me see. (*She looks at the page* PIERCE *has indicated.*) No, I'm afraid not. Too late. (*She returns the book to* PIERCE, *moves above the tapestry and studies it.*) Why *did* this particular figure have to be torn away ? Whatever he is, he must have the right boots.

PIERCE (*adding her book to the pile on the desk*). Sandals might be correct if he were a priest.

SARAT. He has no tonsure.

(MARY *enters* L. *She carries a book and some sewing.*)

MARY (*moving* L. *of* SARAT). I think we've found your book. (*She hands the book to* SARAT.) Page fifty-six, where the marker is.

SARAT (*taking the book and reading the title*). Fifteenth-century Embroidery. Sister, what a find. (*She sits on the stool above the frame, opens the book at the marked page and compares the illustrations with the tapestry.*) Courtier, groom, processional dress—falconer— yes, why didn't I think of it ? (*She looks up at* MARY *with a smile.*) Thank you, Sister.

(*The telephone rings.* MARY *moves below the desk, puts her sewing on the back of the chair* L. *of it, and lifts the telephone receiver.*)

MARY (*into the telephone*). Sister Bonaventure . . . Yes, he's here . . . Yes, certainly. (*She replaces the receiver. To* MELLING.) Newlands wants you downstairs, Officer.

MELLING. Shall I take these books back to the library for you ?

MARY. I should be grateful.

(MELLING *collects the books together and exits* L. PIERCE *picks up the paper from the window seat, moves to the chair* R. *of the stove, sits and starts to read.* SARAT *rises, moves to the desk, sits at it, and*

*starts to sketch, copying the illustration from the book. MARY moves
R. of the desk, then above it to the bookcase and picks up her
workbasket.)*

(*To* SARAT.)   Sister Agnes is getting most enthusiastic about starting
the embroidery.

SARAT.   I should like to see it complete. (*Her pencil pauses for a
second.*)   I've not finished my part yet. (*She resumes sketching.*)

MARY (*moving* L. *of* SARAT).   You will. (*She stands watching*
SARAT.)   How quick and sure your strokes are.   It must be wonderful to be creative.

SARAT.   Sometimes it's hell.   Things just won't work out.   And
sometimes everything goes perfectly, and you feel you're God.

(MARY *moves to the chair* L. *of the desk, picks up her sewing and sits.
She then places her workbasket on the* L. *end of the desk and starts
to sew.*)

MARY.   The newspaper reports said you sketched every day
throughout the trial.

SARAT (*without looking up*).   I must have drawn everything in
sight.   The Judge, Counsel—even the ushers.   The trouble was
they all kept getting the same face.

MARY.   Whose ?

SARAT.   Jason's.

MARY.   Was he so much in your mind ?

SARAT.   I couldn't help thinking how he'd have enjoyed the situation.   He could draw too, you know, in a facile showy way.   He
couldn't be bothered to learn properly. (*She pauses.*)   Poor devil.
He made such a mess of his life.   Things might have been so
different.

MARY (*intent on her sewing*).   He made your life intensely unhappy.
Yet you have this—this depth of pity for him.

SARAT.   People can't help the way they're made, can they ?
Jason's make-up was completely physical.   When he became help-
less, he had absolutely nothing left.   You should understand, Sister.
It must be terrible to have no spiritual resources.

MARY (*quietly*).   Yes.   Was he so very bad ?

SARAT.   Probably only the normal male appetite to start with.
But he had an odd perverted streak of mental cruelty which drove
him too far.   Poor Jason.   We had some grim interludes.

MARY.   Such as the royal case in Florida ?

(SARAT *puts down her pencil.*)

SARAT.   Who on earth told you that ?   No-one knew . . .

MARY.   Martha overheard you talking.   The words stuck in her
mind.

SARAT.   Martha ?

MARY.   Would it distress you to tell me ?

SARAT. No. (*She starts to sketch again.*) About eight years ago
I was working on a commission in Florida. Jason followed me—as
usual. He got mixed up with a girl, called Bee Royal—a solitary
intense fool—God help her. When he let her down, as he always   ·
let everyone down, she gassed herself.

MARY. Was there trouble afterwards ?

SARAT (*laughing shortly*). Jason didn't even appear at the inquest.
She wrote him a pathetic raving letter, but she also sent one to the
coroner, saying she made no charges against anyone, but the person
concerned would be haunted by his conscience for the rest of his
life. (*She erases part of her sketch with a quick movement.*) She
didn't know Jason. (*She resumes sketching.*) I wouldn't have known
much about it myself, but she sent me a letter, too.

MARY. Why you ?

SARAT. She seemed to think we were of one blood, and therefore
one character. Actually, I only met her twice. For a man of his
temperament, Jason knew how to be discreet. (*She rises, picks up
her sketch, moves to the stool above the tapestry and sits.*) Let's talk
about something else, shall we ? What are you making ? (*She
props the sketch against the frame and commences to paint the tapestry.*)

MARY. A christening robe for the Grimes' baby. Poor Mrs
Grimes is so bewildered at having a boy that she hasn't the slightest
idea what to call him. Any suggestions ?

SARAT. Personally, I prefer plain names. John or Charles would
be nice. What's your choice ?

MARY (*after a short pause ; quietly*). I rather like David.

(SARAT *puts down her brush. For a moment she sits very still, then
turns on her stool towards* MARY.)

SARAT. You've been asked to approach me, haven't you ?

MARY. Yes.

SARAT (*directly*). And how do you feel about it ?

MARY. I'm divided between my desire to help you, and my
equally strong opinion that it's your own personal business.

SARAT. I wish I'd had you to talk to in the beginning. (*She takes
up her brush and resumes painting.*)

MARY (*putting her sewing on the desk*). Talk to me now, Sarat.
Why won't you see him or write to him ?

SARAT. Haven't I done enough ? His career is spoilt—probably
the rest of his life affected—just because he knew me.

MARY. I'm sure he doesn't see it in that way. If you met—
once more . . .

SARAT. No. I couldn't bear it.

MARY. But if he wishes . . .

SARAT. I can't help that. (*She sweeps her brush across the canvas.
Desperately.*) Don't you understand—can't you realize—if I saw
him again—spoke to him—I should go up like straw ?

MARY (*gently*). I'm so sorry. I was wrong to speak of it. (*She resumes sewing.*)

SARAT (*looking at the canvas*). Damn. I've smudged it. That's what comes of talking while you work. Pass me that rag, will you, Sister ?

(MARY *rises, picks up the rag from her desk, moves to* R. *of* SARAT, *gives it to her, then stands watching.*)

MARY (*suddenly*). Sarat . . .

SARAT. It's best like this, Sister. Please don't try and persuade me otherwise.

(MARY *moves to the chair* L. *of the desk, sits, picks up her sewing and resumes work.*)

MARY. If you must torment yourself, need you do it to him also ?

(SARAT, *with her brush and the rag in her hands, rises and moves above the desk.*)

SARAT (*abruptly*). He'll forget. Men do. (*She dips her brush in the jar of water to clean it.*)

MARY (*looking up quietly*). Yes. They do. (*Half to herself.*) But—women go on remembering.

(SARAT *mechanically wipes her brush. Her head is bent and she is lost in her own memories. She does not comprehend* MARY'S *words.*)

SARAT (*slowly*). I hope he won't—forget everything. I suppose everyone imagines her own love affair to be the most wonderful thing that ever happened. (*Quietly.*) I know mine was. (*She stands very still above the desk.*) We were so—so mentally complete. Our minds struck sparks. (*She pauses.*) I've lived it over and over again since. Particularly the little idiotic things. (*Quietly.*) You know. (*She pauses, then cleans her brush again.*)

MARY (*to herself*). I—know.

SARAT. Once, in Paris, we paid three visits to the top of the Eiffel Tower. Once so that he could watch me see the view, once so that I could watch him, and the third time so that we could both see it together.

MARY. I can't think of three better reasons.

SARAT. Then someone said : " But you could have done all that in one visit." And we just looked at each other. We simply hadn't thought of it. That's how crazy we were, and how close. (*She moves to the stool above the frame, sits and resumes painting.*) I'm glad I told you. It's made it fresh in my mind again.

(MARY *sits looking straight in front of her, her thoughts far away for the moment.* MELLING *enters* L. *and crosses to* PIERCE, *who puts down the newspaper and rises.* MELLING *and* PIERCE *speak together inaudibly.* SARAT *glances at them, then resumes painting.*)

(*To* MELLING.)   Now, Officer, we can't have you making overtures to Miss Pierce while you're on duty.

(MELLING *moves quietly to* R. *of* SARAT, PIERCE *to* L. *of her.*)

MELLING (*quietly*).   Is there much more to do ?
SARAT (*without looking up ; concentrating on a tricky curve*).   Not very much.

(*Suddenly, instinctively,* MARY *rises.   There is a pause.* SARAT *stops working, looks at* PIERCE, *then at* MELLING.)

(*Evenly.*)   Why do you ask ?
MELLING.   Now, Miss Carn . . .
SARAT (*in the same tone*).   Why do you ask ?
MELLING.   I thought you'd like to finish if you could.   You've been very co-operative so far and . . .
SARAT.   For God's sake come to the point.
MELLING.   Newlands has made some sort of connection with the telephone wires.   We contacted a nearby house and finally Norwich. (*Quietly.*)   I've spoken to the Governor.   They're sending out a police launch.   (*He glances at his wrist-watch.*)   I should say maybe another three hours.

(*There is a pause, then* SARAT *drops her brush on the stool* R. *of the frame and rises abruptly.* MELLING *and* PIERCE *steady her quickly, both hands on her elbows.* MARY *puts her sewing on the desk.*)

Take it easy, Miss Carn.
SARAT.   Thank you, Officer.   Don't worry.   Could you and Miss Pierce—give me a few minutes with Sister—quite alone ?
MELLING.   We'll go out of hearing.   I'm afraid we can't go out of sight.

(*He moves to the door* L., *opens it and glances at* PIERCE, *who exits. He follows her off, leaving the door open.* SARAT *crosses to the window and stands looking out.*)

SARAT (*steadily*).   It had to come, of course.   We knew that.
MARY (*moving below the stove*).   Sarat—would you let me be with you . . . ?
SARAT (*turning and moving above the desk*).   You can do that without leaving here.
MARY.   Yes.   If you wish it.
SARAT.   I've been lucky to get this peaceful interval.   I've had vastly different surroundings, I've completed a piece of work which I think is good.   I've known you—and believe me, that means a great deal.
MARY.   Thank you.
SARAT.   I'm not sentimental, and I don't particularly believe in the power of thought.   But I'll ask Pierce to let you know—and then—if you want to pray or anything . . . (*She suddenly grips the*

*edge of the desk with both hands, and looks down, fighting for control.
To herself.)* Oh, God ! *(She sits in the chair above the desk.)*

(MARY moves quickly to SARAT, *puts her arms around her, and holds
her close.)*

(She leans her head against MARY. *Exhaustedly.)* There's something the Chaplain reads, isn't there ?   I would only see him once—
but he did tell me—and the words were like a roll of drums.
" I am the Resurrection and the Life . . . "

MARY. " I am the Resurrection and the Life, saith the Lord.
He that believeth on Me, though he were dead, yet shall—— "
(She pauses.)

SARAT. Go on.

MARY. " —yet shall he live.   And he that liveth and believeth
on Me, shall never die."   *(Quietly.)*   It *is* like a roll of drums.

(There is a pause. SARAT *moves away from* MARY *and leans on the
desk.)*

SARAT. I've never been religious.

MARY. You mean you've never troubled about the accepted
forms.

SARAT. And I don't want them now.   If this has to happen, why
can't they just be businesslike—and get it over ?

MARY *(moving down* L.C.).   It is thought we need intercession.
(She suddenly raises her hands and covers her face.)

SARAT. Why, Sister—dear Sister Mary—what is it ?

MARY. I would give anything to help you at this moment.   *(She
turns despairingly to* SARAT.)   How can I when I'm as full of doubts
as you are ?

SARAT. You could make a pretence.   You could offer prayers
and platitudes.   *(Simply.)*   Instead, you give me this complete
honesty.

MARY *(in a very low voice).*   Oh, Sarat.

SARAT *(rising and moving to* R. *of* MARY).   Do you know what I've
been afraid of all along ?   Of losing the only thing left to me.   My
personal self-respect.   My pride.   Is that wrong ?

MARY. No.

SARAT *(sitting in the chair* L. *of the desk and facing* MARY).   To go
to pieces at the last moment—disintegrate.   The others are scared
of that, too.   Melling, Pierce, even the Governor.   They don't mention it, but each knows it's in the other's mind.

MARY *(easing to* L. *of* SARAT).   Sarat, you have so much courage.
Don't be afraid any more.

SARAT. That's what I'm trying to tell you—since I've known and
talked to you, I don't think I shall be.   *(She reaches out and holds
MARY's hand.)*   Only—stay with me until we leave—please stay with
me till we leave.

MARY *(holding* SARAT's *hand tightly).*   I will.

SARAT (*after a pause ; rising abruptly*). I must get on.

MARY. Your hands are shaking. You can't possibly work. (*She moves* L. *and calls.*) Officer.

(MELLING *and* PIERCE *enter* L.)

Miss Carn would like to finish her painting. With your permission, I'm going to ask Dr Jeffreys to give her a sedative.

MELLING. Would you like me to go and find him ?

MARY. If you would be so kind. I expect he's in his room.

(MELLING *exits* L. SARAT *leans against the chair* L. *of the desk.* PIERCE *crosses and, not unkindly, puts a hand on* SARAT'S *arm.*)

SARAT (*gently removing* PIERCE'S *hand*). What you and I need, Pierce, is a large brandy and soda.

(*She crosses to the door up* L.C. *and exits.* PIERCE *follows her off.* MARY *moves above the desk.* JOSEPHINE *enters hurriedly* L.)

JOSEPHINE (*breathlessly*). I had to come. Is it right what they say ?

MARY. If you mean—is she going back—yes.

JOSEPHINE (*moving* C.). When ?

MARY. They think in perhaps three hours. (*She sits at her desk.*)

(MELLING *and* JEFFREYS *enter* L. JEFFREYS *carries his bag.*)

MELLING (*as he enters*). Sorry to fetch you down like this, Doctor.

JEFFREYS (*crossing to* L. *of the desk*). It's all right. (*He puts his bag on the* L. *end of the desk.*) I'm only surprised she hasn't broken down before. (*He opens his bag, takes out his stethoscope and moves to the door up* L.C.)

(MELLING *and* JEFFREYS *exit up* L.C.)

JOSEPHINE. Has she—broken down ?

MARY. No. She has more courage than we have. And in her own way—more faith.

(JEFFREYS *enters up* L.C. *His stethoscope hangs around his neck.*)

JEFFREYS (*moving to* L. *of the desk*). What we ought to do is put her right out for twenty-four hours, (*he searches in his bag*) but she insists on finishing that confounded painting. (*He pauses and takes an empty bottle from his bag.*) Damn, I'm out of phenobarbitone. Got any in your cupboard, Sister ? (*He puts the empty bottle on the desk.*)

MARY (*rising*). Yes, Doctor. (*She moves to the bookcase and opens the cupboard.*)

JEFFREYS (*moving to the door up* L.C.). Bring it in to me, will you, please ?

(*He exits up* L.C. JOSEPHINE *moves to the desk and picks up the empty bottle.* MARY *takes two small bottles from the cupboard.*)

JOSEPHINE. An empty bottle is a dreary sight at any time—specially in a doctor's bag. (*She replaces the bottle on the desk.*)

MARY (*moving above the desk*). Here, give him this full one. We can spare it.

(*She gives one bottle to* JOSEPHINE, *then moves to the door up* L.C. *and exits.* JOSEPHINE *opens* JEFFREY'S *bag to put the bottle in it, and shakes her head over the contents.*)

JOSEPHINE (*sorting out the items in the bag and tidying it*). Dear goodness—the clutter the man carries about with him. It's a guid thing I don't carry the tools of my trade. A fine sight I'd look with a couple of saucepans and my iron-bottomed frying pan. (*She puts the piece of folded gauze on the desk.*)

(MARY *enters up* L.C. *and moves above the desk.*)

MARY (*smiling*). You just can't resist tidying people up, can you ? (*She picks up the piece of gauze.*) Now this gauze has got paint on it. (*She opens it out and a newspaper cutting falls out of it.*)

JOSEPHINE. Oh, mercy !

(MARY *picks up the cutting, glances at it, then pauses and reads it.*)

MARY. What on earth . . . ?

JOSEPHINE. What's the matter ?

MARY (*slowly*). It's a cutting from my file. (*She looks at the cutting again, then slips it hurriedly under the blotter.*) Quickly—put everything back.

(JOSEPHINE *hastily repacks the bag.*)

Wait—give me a newspaper—on the window seat—hurry. (*She picks up the scissors.*)

(JOSEPHINE *moves to the window seat, picks up the newspaper and passes it to* MARY, *who hurriedly cuts out a strip of paper about the length of the cutting and rolls it in the gauze. She then puts the gauze in the bag and shuts it. She pauses a moment, glances at the door up* L.C., *then takes the cutting from under her blotter and studies it.*)

JOSEPHINE (*easing to* R. *of the desk*). What's it doing in his bag ?

MARY. I don't—know. (*She pauses.*) Wait a minute—he asked me for that gauze yesterday. The cuttings were on my desk when he folded it.

JOSEPHINE. Aye. He caught that one up and put it in the bag by accident.

MARY. I suppose so. (*She looks at the cutting thoughtfully.*) And yet—I had all the cuttings in a spring clip. (*She looks up.*) I remember—I was at the cupboard—Martha came in and I looked up. He was standing here with the file in his hand, fiddling with the clip. He could have—taken it off.

JOSEPHINE. Not by chance. He'd need to do more than fiddle.

MARY. Then he meant to take it.

JOSEPHINE. Perhaps it's not one of yours.

MARY. Yes. Look—there's the mark of the clip. (*She quickly opens the desk drawer, takes out the bulldog clip and fits it on to the cutting.*) It fits the dents exactly. (*She looks towards the door up* L.C.) Sister Josephine, just what does this mean ?

JOSEPHINE. He didn't want you to study that one too closely. Which one is it ?

MARY (*looking at the cutting*). It's the report of his cross-examination. (*She looks up. Slowly.*) All my cuttings were burnt —or so I thought. There was nothing I could do but resign myself. And now, by some utterly unlooked-for incident, this is returned to me.

JOSEPHINE. Do you think you should harry yourself all over again ? It might be coincidence.

MARY. Perhaps I've been working in the wrong direction. Perhaps this is an indication of the right one.

JOSEPHINE. But why should he bother to take one when the whole lot went in the stove together ?

MARY. He didn't know that would happen. It was Nurse Phillips who told the Reverend Mother about the cuttings.

JOSEPHINE (*suddenly*). Who said she did ?

MARY. Why, no-one. But she must have done.

JOSEPHINE. When did she ever see them ? They weren't on the desk last night. You put them in the drawer before Phillips came in.

MARY. Yes. Who else knew besides you and me ?

JOSEPHINE (*nodding towards the door up* L.C.). He did.

MARY. But surely—he's done everything to help Sarat. And you've forgotten, haven't you ? When it all happened, he was in Norwich.

JOSEPHINE. Yes. No getting over that.

MARY. I want to think. (*She sits at her desk.*) Let me read this through, thoroughly. I may be wrong, but I feel as though . . .

(*She breaks off as the door up* L.C. *opens and* JEFFREYS *enters.* MARY *slides the cutting under the blotter.*)

JEFFREYS (*moving to* L. *of the desk*). I've given her a grain and a half, Sister. (*He puts his stethoscope in his bag.*) Let her have a warm drink in about an hour. (*He closes his bag, picks it up and moves to the door* L.) Whichever way you look at it, this is a wretched business.

(*He exits* L. MARY *and* JOSEPHINE *look at each other, then* MARY *pulls out the cutting and studies it.*)

MARY. But what reason would he have for telling the Reverend Mother about the cuttings ? (*She looks up.*) Could it have been Willy ?

JOSEPHINE. Willy ? (*She turns to the window.*) Och, the puir laddie couldn't read a newspaper well enough to know what it meant. All he worries about in here is whether the sweeties are sticky enough to give him two or three in one.

MARY (*suddenly*). Sister Josephine !

(JOSEPHINE *turns, startled at the tone of* MARY'S *voice.*)

JOSEPHINE. What is it, Sister ?

(MARY *looks at the cutting for a second, then puts it down on the desk.*)

MARY. I must—have been—very stupid.

She looks across at the door L. *as—*

the CURTAIN *falls.*

SCENE 2

SCENE.—*The Great Hall. About three hours later.*
There are signs of recent and hurried occupation. A roll of bedding and three suitcases stand L. *of the staircase. The stool from down* R. *is now* R. *of the armchair* L.C. *The lights have been switched on and a cheerful fire burns in the grate.*

When the CURTAIN *rises, the stage is empty. A bell with a thin but sweet note is ringing off in the distance. After a few moments,* MELLING *enters up* L., *and comes down the stairs, unrolling his shirt sleeves. He moves above the table, picks up his jacket, puts it on and buttons it up. As he does so,* JOSEPHINE *enters down* R. *She carries a full basket, with a white cloth tucked over the top.*

JOSEPHINE (*placing the basket on the* R. *end of the table*). There's a few things—sandwiches and a wee cake. And some preserve—my special apricot with the kernels blanched in it. I'm thinking maybe your cook at the—at Norwich—doesn't get much practice, except at plain food.

MELLING (*moving above the* R. *end of the table*). This is very kind indeed, Sister. (*He turns back the cloth and peers into the basket.*) My word !

JOSEPHINE (*sharply*). Now keep your hands off, young man. It's for the journey, not for pickings beforehand. (*She replaces the cloth.*) The packet on top's for that.

MELLING. We shall be very grateful. Would you give it to Newlands for me ? Tell him to take great care of it and not let it out of his sight.

JOSEPHINE. Aye. (*She picks up the basket, moves down* R., *then stops and turns.*) Officer, will you tell Miss Carn—will you tell her I said good-bye—and God bless her ? (*Her voice breaks on the last words.*)

MELLING (*gently*). Yes, Sister. I will.

JOSEPHINE. There's a wee flask in here with something to keep out the cold. But only for you three, mind. If you start sharing it, you'll only get a toothful.

(*She turns and exits down* R. *The* MOTHER SUPERIOR *enters* L.C. *and moves* L. *of the armchair* L.C. *to the fireplace.*)

MOTHER SUPERIOR (*looking around*). Why—how nice. We're very nearly straight again, thanks to you and Mr Newlands.

MELLING (*easing a little up* C.). It's the least we can do for you, madam, especially in the circumstances. By the way, the Governor will be communicating with you, but when I spoke to him, he mentioned the question of any payment—or donation.

MOTHER SUPERIOR. No, Officer. It is our work to help you. (*She sits in the armchair* L.C.)

(MELLING *glances at his wrist-watch.*)

Your—people—will be here any moment ?

MELLING. Yes. The doctor is coming with us, just as a precaution.

MOTHER SUPERIOR. I think you were wise to suggest it.

MELLING. It was Sister Mary's idea.

MOTHER SUPERIOR. Oh.

MELLING. And *she* also suggested we might wait here for the last half hour. Easier to get out. The last moments may be—awkward.

(JEFFREYS *enters down* R. *He carries his bag and has his overcoat over his arm.*)

JEFFREYS (*putting his overcoat on the sideboard*). The water is still pretty high. (*He puts his bag on the* L. *end of the table.*) Think we shall get into that launch without a ducking, Officer ?

MELLING. I've told them to try round where the main gate would be. Then we can more or less step down from the cloisters.

JEFFREYS. I hope you're right. (*He crosses to the fireplace.*) Good evening, Reverend Mother. (*He stands with his back to the fire.*)

(MARTHA *enters down* R.)

MARTHA (*uncomfortably*). Please, Reverend Mother.

MOTHER SUPERIOR. If it's not important, Martha, I should prefer to wait.

MARTHA (*moving* C.). Well, you see, tes that awkward. About Miss Carn . . .

MOTHER SUPERIOR. Yes ?

MARTHA. Tes Willy. He knows she's goin' and he've got some flowers for her. And nuthin' will suit him but to give them himself.

(WILLY *enters slowly* R. *He is wearing his overalls. He carries a tiny bunch of snowdrops.*)

MOTHER SUPERIOR (*rising*).   Come here, Willy.

(WILLY *crosses to* R. *of the* MOTHER SUPERIOR.   *He is puzzled by the general atmosphere, and looks uncertainly from one to the other.*)

Your mother tells me those flowers are for Miss Carn.

WILLY.   For Miss Sarat, ma'am, yes.   But they woon't let me give . . .

(SARAT, MARY *and* PIERCE *enter up* L.   SARAT *wears her caped coat across her shoulders with dignity.*   MARY *carries her workbasket, her needlework, and a large book.*   SARAT *hesitates at the top of the stairs as she sees the group below, all looking up at her.*   *Then* MARY *puts a hand under* SARAT'S *arm and they come down the stairs together.*   PIERCE *waits on the gallery.*   MARY *pauses on the bottom step.*   SARAT *moves to* R. *of* WILLY.)

Miss Sarat . . .   (*He goes to offer the flowers, then looks behind him at the* MOTHER SUPERIOR.)   May I ?

(*The* MOTHER SUPERIOR *nods.*)

(*He turns to* SARAT.)   Miss Sarat—I—I thought you'd like these.   I bin growin' un in kitchen window box, but Sister Josephine said I could pick un.

(*Without speaking,* SARAT *takes the flowers and holds them up to her face.*)

(*Anxiously.*)   They've no smell, Miss Sarat—only just fresh and clean like.

MELLING.   Miss Carn's very pleased.   But we've got things to do.   Say good-bye, now, there's a good lad.

WILLY.   Good-bye, Miss Sarat.   (*Slowly.*)   It'll be strange at the Grape House wi'out you sitting paintin' them big pictures.   (*He crosses below the table towards the arch down* R.)

SARAT.   Willy.   (*She moves to* L. *of him.*)

(WILLY *stops and turns.*   SARAT *holds out her hand.*   *He looks at it, wipes his own on his overalls, then shakes hands with her.*   MARTHA *takes his arm and they exit together down* R.   SARAT *abruptly turns her back, her head bent down to the flowers in her hand.*   *The* MOTHER SUPERIOR *moves above* SARAT.)

MOTHER SUPERIOR (*almost inaudibly*).   God be with you.   (*She crosses herself.*)

(SARAT *breaks quickly to the pillar up* R., *and stands with her left hand on it, her back to the audience, her head bowed.*   *The* MOTHER SUPERIOR *moves to the door* L. *and exits.*   MARY *crosses to the sideboard and puts down the book.*   *She then crosses to the armchair* L.C., *puts the workbasket on the stool* R. *of it, sits in the armchair and starts to sew.*   MELLING *moves to the chair* R. *of the table and sits.* PIERCE *comes down the stairs and moves above the table. She pauses a moment and looks at* SARAT. SARAT *straightens up, turns, then moves to the chair above the table and sits. She rests her hands on the table, turning over the little bunch of flowers.* PIERCE *then moves and sits on the bench below the table, with her back to the audience. There is an awkward pause.*)

MELLING ⎱ (*together*). ⎰Don't you think . . . ?
JEFFREYS ⎰   ⎱Perhaps we should . . .

                    (*They break off.*)

SARAT (*laughing*).   Not a very good conversational effort, gentlemen.   But thank you for trying.   Have you a pin, Sister ?
MARY.   I think so.   (*She searches in her workbasket.*)   You want a fairly big one.   (*She holds out a pin.*)   Here.

(JEFFREYS *takes the pin from* MARY, *crosses to* L. *of* SARAT *and gives it to her.* SARAT *fastens the flowers to her coat.*)

They look brave against the colour.
SARAT.   Yes.   (*She leans back in her chair. Her fingers tap restlessly on the table edge. She looks at her fingers.*)   Now that design is finished, I feel strange with no brush or pencil.
JEFFREYS (*taking his cigarette case and matches from his pocket*). Cigarette ?
SARAT.   Not now, thanks.

(JEFFREYS *moves to the pillar up* R., *leans against it and lights a cigarette for himself.*)

MARY (*rising and moving to* L. *of* SARAT).   Miss Pierce, in the sideboard drawer you'll find a pack of cards.   The night nurses keep them there for slack intervals.

(PIERCE *rises, moves to the sideboard, gets the cards from the drawer, returns below the table, hands the cards across it to* SARAT *and resumes her seat.*)

They think I don't know and I don't say anything because they'd only have to find another hiding place.
SARAT.   It wouldn't surprise me to hear you'd taken a hand with them.
MARY (*smiling*).   Would it surprise you to know I used to play a very good hand of bridge ?
SARAT.   Not in the least.   (*She lays some cards out, one by one.*) Knave, Queen, King.
MARY.   Didn't someone once say—all the human passions on bits of pasteboard ?   (*She returns to her seat in the armchair and resumes her sewing.*)
SARAT.   One doesn't imagine human passions quite so flat and abstract.   (*She starts to build a house of cards.*)

MARY. No. Considering the havoc they make of our lives.

JEFFREYS. That's a fallacious argument. Not all people are subject to excessive feeling.

MARY. Surely it's in all of us to feel deeply. If not from choice, then from force of circumstances.

JEFFREYS. In which case it becomes a simple matter of self-control.

MARY. Except that the basic human passions are in the mind, and that is not simple. Don't you agree, Doctor?

JEFFREYS. I don't even think it simple to enumerate these—these basic passions, as you call them.

SARAT. Heavens, nothing easier. Jealousy, greed, fear ...

MARY. Anger and desire.

SARAT. And the end of them all is destruction. (*She flicks over the house of cards.*) Of the individual. Of the world.

MARY. Not inevitably.

SARAT. Invariably. I'll have that cigarette, please, Doctor.

(JEFFREYS *moves to* R. *of* SARAT, *gives her a cigarette and lights it.* PIERCE *picks up the cards and starts to play patience.*)

MARY. You know, we come in contact with much that is strange and disturbing. (*She pauses as she threads her needle.*) I myself was once shown most vividly just how far jealousy and frustration could go.

SARAT. Tell us about it.

(JEFFREYS *moves above the armchair* L.C., *then down* L. *of it to the stool below the fireplace, where he sits smoking, with his back to the audience.*)

JEFFREYS (*as he moves*). Don't you think we might talk about something—well, less ...

SARAT. The weather? The floods? Politics? No. I'd like to listen to Sister. (*She looks pointedly at* MELLING.) If you don't mind.

MELLING. If Sister doesn't mind.

MARY. It's the oldest story in the world. The love of a man for a woman.

SARAT (*lightly, but with bitterness*). A good woman, I hope.

MARY. At the worst, a weak one. Through the influence of another man, she died. And the first man, who must have loved her very dearly, allowed his grief and bitterness to drive him beyond normal control.

SARAT. He killed himself?

MARY. He killed the other man.

SARAT. And then the law killed *him*—legally. (*She crushes out her cigarette angrily in the ashtray on the table in front of her.*) Well, well, how just and merciful.

PIERCE (*quietly*). Miss Carn.

SARAT (*reaching over and moving some of* PIERCE's *cards*). Nine, ten—put that five on the six there, Pierce, and don't excite your basic passions. (*She pauses, then puts her hand on* PIERCE's.) There —I'm sorry.

MELLING. It's certainly an old story. We've heard it often enough, haven't we, Miss Pierce?

MARY. It has an unusual ending. You see—the law didn't know.

SARAT. You mean—he got away with it? He must have been clever.

MARY. He'd planned so carefully, detail by detail. I think he'd forgotten everything but his obsession for revenge.

MELLING (*abruptly*). Miss Carn, what about three-handed whist?

SARAT. Don't side-track, Officer. I want to hear the end.

JEFFREYS. Probably a criminal lunatic asylum.

MARY. If his guilt could be proved.

SARAT. Why couldn't it? The law can prove anything. (*She laughs.*) I learned that at the Assizes.

MELLING. Now please, Miss Carn.

SARAT. Sister, what makes you think this man so—so safe?

JEFFREYS. Obviously he has the finest possible defence.

SARAT. And what would that be?

JEFFREYS. A perfect alibi.

MELLING (*shaking his head*). A perfect alibi means perfect innocence.

MARY. I see you are a purist, Officer. Dr Jeffreys should have said—unshakable, not perfect.

SARAT. How?

MARY. He was some miles away when the crime was committed.

JEFFREYS. Impossible.

MARY (*bending over her sewing*). A mine may be exploded from a distance.

SARAT. Murder by remote control. Was this man by any chance a scientist?

MARY. A specialist in his own profession.

MELLING (*rising*). Sister . . .

(JEFFREYS *rises, throws his cigarette end into the fire, then moves up* L. *of the armchair* L.C. *to the stairs.*)

JEFFREYS. Officer, how about going up to the tower and having a look out? I could do with a breath of air. (*He glances meaningly at* SARAT *behind her back.*)

(MARY *takes a pair of scissors from her workbasket.*)

MELLING. Good idea, sir. Miss Carn, would you care . . .

MARY (*cutting a silk thread*). Oh! (*She drops her scissors, and holds her left hand.*)

SARAT (*rising quickly*). You've cut yourself—mind that silk—quick. (*She takes* MARY'S *sewing and puts it on the table.*)

MARY. It's only a scratch. Have you some plaster in your case, Doctor ?

JEFFREYS (*moving to the table*). Yes, of course. (*He picks up his case, transfers it to the stool* R. *of the armchair, and opens it.*)

SARAT (*looking at the sewing*). No harm done. (*She moves above the armchair to* L. *of* MARY.) How about your hand, Sister ? (*She looks at* MARY'S *hand.*) It's a nasty deep cut.

JEFFREYS. Let me see. (*He looks at* MARY'S *hand.*) Nothing very much. I'll just cover it.

(SARAT *moves to her seat above the table and sits.* MELLING *resumes his seat* R. *of the table.* JEFFREYS *takes a roll of surgical tape from his bag, moves above the armchair to* L. *of it, kneels* L.. *of* MARY *and binds the cut.* MARY *reaches out with her right hand and takes a roll of red binding out of the bag.*)

MARY. Isn't this the plaster ? Oh—chemist's sealing tape. (*She reads.*) Abel Harmer.

(JEFFREYS *pinches her finger.*)

(*Involuntarily.*) Oh !

JEFFREYS. I'm sorry.

MARY (*replacing the tape in the bag*). Harmer. That's the chemist in the village, isn't it ? The one who made up the prescription for Miss Carn's brother ?

JEFFREYS. Yes. Keep your hand still, Sister.

MARY. I think you told me you collected the tablets once every three weeks, checked them with Harmer, and took them to Miss Carn.

JEFFREYS. You're not being very kind or tactful to mention it, are you ? Pass me the scissors, please.

(MARY *takes the scissors from the bag and passes them to* JEFFREYS.)

SARAT. If you mean on my account, I'm past caring. Why do you ask, Sister ?

(JEFFREYS *cuts off the tape.*)

MARY. Because I know how careful one must be with drugs. A five-grain barbiturate tablet may bear a fatal resemblance to a five-grain tablet of aspirin.

(JEFFREYS *rises.*)

Thank you, Doctor, that's comfortable. (*She rises and moves to* L. *of* SARAT. *Quietly.*) I use the word fatal, advisedly.

JEFFREYS. Officer, I do think we should ask Sister to stop this discussion or, as a medical man I can't answer for Miss Carn's reactions.

SARAT. My reaction at the moment is avid curiosity.

MARY. I wish you'd been a little more curious about that last phial of tablets. It is just possible that one—the fourth—may have been a fraction larger than the others.

(JEFFREYS *drops the roll of tape and the scissors into the open bag.*)

JEFFREYS (*moving to the stairs*). Sister, you're talking absolute nonsense. I'm going upstairs.

(MARY *moves to* R. *of the stairs.*)

MELLING (*rising ; sensibly*). There's really nothing to be gained by all this, Sister.

SARAT (*abruptly*). Why should that fourth tablet have been larger ?

MARY. Because I think it contained the equivalent of three ordinary ones.

(JEFFREYS *breaks a step to* L. *The others stare at* MARY.)

In other words, the necessary overdose could have been put into one tablet. (*She pauses.*)

(*No-one moves.*)

(*She moves to* L. *of* SARAT.) You see ? (*In dialect.*) Two or three in one. (*In her normal voice.*) Like Willy's sweets. The tablets were packed singly in a glass phial. According to its position, the overdose would be given on a certain day during twenty-one days. Twenty-one days during which the person who had prepared that overdose could be any distance away.

JEFFREYS (*suddenly*). Officer—for heaven's sake . . . (*He breaks off, moves down* L. *of the armchair and stands in front of the fire.*)

MARY (*moving a little down* L.C. *and facing* JEFFREYS). Sarat—who first brought you down to Denzil St David ?

SARAT. The murals for the church. (*She pauses.*) Dr Jeffreys.

MARY. Who prescribed those tablets and delivered them to you ?

SARAT. Dr Jeffreys.

MARY. Who actually suggested those tablets should be analysed ?

SARAT. Dr . . .

JEFFREYS (*furiously*). I won't stand by and listen to this.

MELLING (*moving above the table*). Sister, one moment. Are you making definite accusations against Dr Jeffreys ?

MARY. I am asking you to place certain information in the proper quarter for consideration.

JEFFREYS. But . . .

MELLING. Please, sir. Sister, will you be specific ?

MARY (*turning and facing* MELLING). I would like to suggest Dr Jeffreys brought Miss Carn here, knowing her brother would follow. Jason's high blood pressure and lack of self-control would make it easy for anyone with medical knowledge to induce a stroke.

(*She turns to* JEFFREYS.)   I myself am not altogether ignorant of certain drugs.

JEFFREYS.   I warn you to be careful.

MARY.   I further suggest Dr Jeffreys collected that phial of tablets, emptied it, and refilled it so that the last two tablets were aspirins and the fourth the prepared one.   He then resealed the phial with Harmer's tape, delivered it and went to Norwich—knowing exactly when the prepared tablet would be given.

SARAT (*involuntarily*).   By me.

MARY (*still looking at* JEFFREYS).   By you.

SARAT (*in a whisper*).   Oh, God !

MELLING.   This is purely supposition, Sister.   But you had better make a statement in writing, and I'll take it with me.

MARY.   I will.   Meanwhile, Miss Carn is entitled to see her solicitor at once.

JEFFREYS.   But this whole thing—it's *fantastic*.

MELLING.   I'm inclined to agree, sir.   But in a capital charge, the merest indication of doubt must be properly investigated.   You do see that ?

JEFFREYS (*impatiently*).   Of course, of course.   I'll talk to the Governor.   He'll quite understand Sister Mary has allowed the emotional circumstances to carry her away.

MARY (*moving to the armchair* L.C.).   I think it only fair to warn you that I am not entirely relying on supposition or emotional circumstances.   (*She sits.*)

MELLING (*moving to* R. *of* MARY).   I did ask you to be specific.

JEFFREYS.   Officer, are you seriously going to listen to this wild story ?

MELLING (*calmly*).   Having gone so far, sir, we'd best get it clear, don't you think ?

JEFFREYS.   But in fairness to Miss Carn . . .

MELLING.   In fairness to yourself.   Yes, Sister ?

MARY.   You may know I made a collection of cuttings about the trial.   They were burnt.   Some time afterwards, by chance, I found one.   (*She takes a newspaper cutting from her pocket.*)   I knew it for one of mine because of the clip marks.   It must have been taken from my file deliberately.   (*She hands the cutting to* MELLING.)

MELLING (*examining the cutting*).   It's the report of Dr Jeffrey's evidence.   (*He looks at* MARY.)   Where did you find it ?

MARY.   In Dr Jeffrey's bag.

MELLING.   Was it in your bag, sir ?

JEFFREYS.   If so, she put it there.   (*He moves above the armchair* L.C.)   Officer, surely you understand ?   This solitary life—they get strange fancies—we know Sister's taken this business to heart—but . . .

MELLING.   Just leave it to me, sir.   We'll straighten things out much quicker.

MARY.   If you look in the bag, you'll find a cutting I substituted, wrapped up in some gauze.   It's cut in the middle of two columns and makes no sense at all.

MELLING.   Well, let's see, shall we ?   Do you mind, sir ?   (*He carries the open bag and puts it on the* L. *end of the table.*)

JEFFREYS (*moving to* L. *of* MELLING ; *impatiently*).   But she just said she put it there.

(MELLING *takes the cutting out of the gauze, glances at it and puts it on the table.*)

MELLING.   You're quite right, Sister.   But that doesn't prove much, does it ?

MARY.   Not by itself.   You might take out that little roll of sealing tape with Harmer's name on it.

(MELLING *takes the roll of red tape from the bag and puts it with the cutting on the table.*)

JEFFREYS.   That doesn't prove anything, either.

MARY.   And the other cutting.

(MELLING *puts the first cutting with the second on the table.*)

MELLING (*shutting the bag*).   Why do you suppose it was taken from your file ?

MARY.   So that I shouldn't study the biographical details too closely.   And note two significant facts.

JEFFREYS.   Well ?

MARY.   First, that about eight years ago you visited America.

JEFFREYS.   What's so strange about America ?

MARY.   There's a State there called Florida.

(SARAT *rises suddenly and stands staring at* JEFFREYS.)

(*To* MELLING.)   Will you ask Miss Carn what that conveys to her ?

MELLING.   Well, Miss Carn ?

SARAT (*still staring at* JEFFREYS ; *hoarsely*).   My brother ...   (*Her voice breaks for a moment.*)   About eight years ago—my brother was responsible for the death of a girl there.

MARY.   What was her name ?

SARAT.   She called herself—Bee Royal.

MARY.   You knew her, I think, Doctor ?

JEFFREYS (*moving above the armchair to the fireplace*).   I've nevei heard of her.   I've not the least idea what you're talking about.

MARY.   The second fact in the cutting told me you were once very prominent in your profession—that you are the author of a standard textbook on congenital diseases.

JEFFREYS.   I don't see what bearing my literary achievements ...

MARY.   I felt that a man of your former distinction might be mentioned in some book of reference.

SARAT.   Sister ...

MARY (*quietly*).   Miss Pierce, would you fetch that book from the sideboard, please ?

(PIERCE *rises, moves to the sideboard and picks up the book.*)

And give it to Mr Melling.

(PIERCE *moves below the table to* MELLING, *hands him the book, then eases a little* R.)

(*To* MELLING.)   You'll find an entry under Dr Jeffreys' name.   The place is marked.   Please read anything relevant.

MELLING (*opening the book and reading*).   " Leslie Jordan Jeffreys, M.D., F.R.C.P., F.R.C.S., Cambridge and London.   Born nineteen hundred and . . . "

JEFFREYS (*angrily*).   This is *ridiculous*——

MELLING.   Now look here, sir—be reasonable.   (*He drops the book on to the table and moves to* R. *of the armchair* L.C.)

(SARAT *sits in the chair above the table and studies the book.*)

JEFFREYS (*ignoring the interruption*).   —it's a preposterous idea. God damn it—there isn't a sound argument in the whole thing. Dragging me in on the strength of some guesswork about tablets— which can't be proved medically— (*he moves above the armchair to* L. *of* SARAT) a cutting which doesn't mean a thing—and the fact that eight years ago in America, some hysterical red-head killed herself.

MARY.   How did you know she had red hair ?

(*There is dead silence for a moment.*)

JEFFREYS (*turning and looking at* MARY).   Why—you said so.

MARY.   I didn't mention it.   (*Quietly.*)   I didn't know.

(SARAT *rises suddenly with the book in her hand.*)

SARAT (*reading breathlessly*).   " Nineteen hundred and thirty-four —married—Beatrice Royal."

(JEFFREYS *makes a quick decisive movement to the table and catches at the book in* SARAT'S *hands.   For a moment they face each other, then* SARAT *lets go of the book and sits.* JEFFREYS *drops the book on to the table with a little thud.   For a moment no-one speaks.* MELLING *starts to make a move forward, but* MARY *stops him with a gesture.*)

(*At last, still breathlessly.*)   Was she—your wife ?

(JEFFREYS *stands looking down at* SARAT. *Except that his hands are shaking, he is very quiet.*)

JEFFREYS.   Yes.   Until your damned brother came into her life.

MELLING (*quickly*).   I must warn you, sir—don't say any more.

(JEFFREYS *turns up* R., *brushing past* MELLING.   *He takes a long striding walk to the door up* R. *and back again to* L. *of* SARAT.)

JEFFREYS. She'd been restless for some years. I was absorbed in my work. I didn't realize. She took a holiday alone—in America.

MELLING. Look here, sir . . .

JEFFREYS (*ignoring the interruption*). I didn't know she'd used her maiden name there. She wrote me a bitter letter about you both. When I received it, she'd been dead some time. (*He moves above the armchair, then down* L. *of it to the fireplace.*) I went out there and checked. I watched you two. I've watched and planned for eight years. (*Slowly.*) I was always too ambitious. I should have been content to let Jason suffer (*his voice rises, but he controls it*) knowing I could let him linger or snuff him out—just as I wished.

SARAT (*desperately*). Don't—please !

JEFFREYS (*moving to* L. *of* SARAT). You were responsible for your own part, Sarat. That day you appealed to me—those damaging remarks you made—with Martha passing in and out. I remember wondering just how soon it would be all round the village—and then I saw the whole thing vividly—because while you talked, you were turning an ordinary bottle of aspirin over and over in your hand.

SARAT (*crying out*). But why me ? Wasn't it sufficient that Jason should suffer ?

JEFFREYS (*bitterly*). Men don't suffer like women do. I wanted another woman to suffer the torments she must have suffered before she died—died alone.

SARAT. Don't—don't !

MELLING (*moving above* SARAT'S *chair*). Doctor . . .

JEFFREYS. But now— (*he turns to* MARY) thanks to Sister Mary— it just shows what can be done with a little luck and a lot of faith— or is it the other way round ?

(*Voices are heard off.* JEFFREYS *stops speaking and listens. There is a sound of hailing as if from a boat, and the bell clangs for a moment, with general sounds of bustle and excitement.*)

PIERCE. That sounds like our people.

MELLING (*moving to* R. *of the table*). I did warn you not to say so much, Doctor.

JEFFREYS. I'm not sorry. The main thing is that Jason's dead. And—if your theology is correct, Sister—in everlasting torment. (*Quietly.*) Eternity is a long time, and I hope he burns through every endless second.

MARY (*rising and facing* JEFFREYS ; *gently*). The mercy of God is also eternal. And His compassion equally endless.

VOICE (*off* R. ; *calling*). Melling—hi, Melling !

JEFFREYS (*shrugging his shoulders*). Perhaps. Because after all, Sarat— (*he turns to her*) you won't hang.

(SARAT *flinches away from him.*)

(*Suddenly.*) And—neither shall I. (*He turns suddenly and races up the stairs.*)

(SARAT *rises.*)

MELLING (*rushing after* JEFFREYS). All right—leave it to me.

(JEFFREYS *exits up* L. *and slams the heavy door in* MELLING'S *face.* MARY *hurries to* R. *of the stairs.*)

(*He thrusts at the door.*) Locked the other side. (*He moves back a step.*) Look out. (*He throws his weight against the door.*)

MARY. You can't—it's solid. (*She moves above the table.*) Miss Pierce—get Newlands.

(PIERCE *exits hurriedly down* R. MARY *starts to follow her, then stops and moves back again above the table.* MELLING *runs down the stairs, hurries to the door up* R., *flings it open and exits to* L. *The daylight floods the room.* MARY *steps out of the door up* R. *on to the small paved terrace. She stands looking up and off* L., *her hands gripped together in front of her.* SARAT *moves to the armchair* L.C., *and leans against it, her face hidden against her arms.*)

MELLING (*off ; calling*). He's on the long gallery—he's making for the tower.

(*There is noise and confusion in the background.* MARY *stands framed in the doorway. She turns her head as if watching someone cross from* L. *to* R. *Suddenly, she flinches. Her hands cover her eyes. The noise off ceases.* SARAT *is quite rigid and does not move.*)

(*He cries out.*) God ! (*He rushes past from* L. *to* R. *above* MARY.)

(*There is a pause. Then* MARY *slowly raises her head. She looks off* R., *turns to face the audience, quietly crosses herself, and re-enters the room, leaving the door open behind her.*)

MARY. Sarat.
(SARAT *does not move.*)

(*She moves to* R. *of* SARAT. *Quietly.*) Sarat.

(SARAT *turns and stares for a moment at* MARY. *Suddenly she steps forward, drops to her knees, clings to* MARY *and breaks into tearing anguished sobs.* MARY *puts her arms around* SARAT, *and her sobs quieten slightly.*)

(*She raises her head. A great radiance comes into her face. Holding* SARAT *tightly in her arms, she recites the opening lines of the Magnificat.*) Magnificat anima mea Dominum, et exaltavit spiritus meus in Deo salutari meo . . .

CURTAIN

FURNITURE AND PROPERTY LIST

ACT I

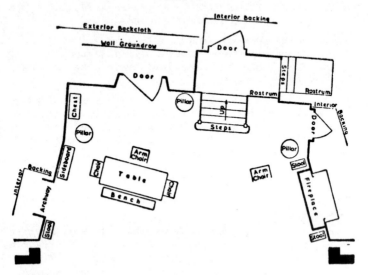

On Stage.

Sideboard. *On it :* telephone, brass bowl.

In drawer · pack of cards with three top cards arranged Knave, Queen, King.

Oak chest.

Pedestal. *On it :* statue of Virgin and Child.

Red lamp.

High-backed armchair.

3 coffin-stools.

Rush mat.

Fire-basket. *In it :* logs.

Firedogs.

Fire-irons.

Ebony crucifix (*over fireplace*).

Refectory table.

3 chairs.

Bench.

2 sets electric candle wall brackets.

2 iron lantern electric fittings.

Light switches (*above fireplace*).

Notice, " TO HOSPITAL. STAFF ONLY ".

Set.

On table : linen table mats, book, newspaper, basket of bread rolls, box of
  matches, ashtray, bowl of fruit, dirty plate, knife, fork, cup and saucer.
  2 table napkins. *At* R. *end :* clean knife and fork, clean cup and saucer.
Electric fittings switched off.
Fire on.

Off Stage.

Tray. *On it :* plate with omelette under a dish-cover, jug of coffee
  (JOSEPHINE).
Basket of logs (WILLY).
Tapestry, newspapers (MARY).
Attaché case. *In it :* stethoscope, bottles, papers, etc. (JEFFREYS).
Tray. *On it :* 2 bowls hot soup, two spoons (MARY).
2 pairs black shoes (BRENT).
Newspaper (BRENT).

Personal.

BRENT : peanuts.
PHILLIPS : fob watch.
JOSEPHINE · knitting.
SARAT : cigarettes.

ACT II

SCENE 1

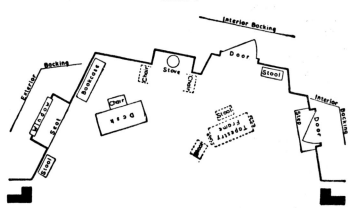

On Stage.

Bookcase.   *On top shelves :* books.

        On bottom shelf : brass box with sweets, microscope, work-basket with cottons, scissors, safety pins and needles.

        On top shelf of cupboard : newspaper lining, bottles, roll of surgical gauze, tray of microscope slides.

        On bottom shelf of cupboard : newspaper lining, boxes, books wrapped in local newspaper.

Desk.   *On it :* telephone, inkstand, eraser, pens, pencils, blotting paper, ashtray, letter tray with letters, folders, penknife, notebook.

        In left-hand drawer : matches, steel tape, scissors.

        In right-hand drawer : typing paper.

        In right-hand second drawer : newspaper cuttings in bulldog clip.

        In right-hand third drawer : drawing paper.

Waste-paper basket.

Upright chair.

2 stools.

Slow-combustion stove.

Mat.

Window seat cushion.

Crucifix (*over stove*).

2 sets electric candle wall brackets.

Set.

Tapestry (with a large hole in it) on stool up L.

MELLING'S jacket on stool up L.

Vase of daffodils on R. end of desk.

Fire on.

Electric fittings on.

Off Stage.

Bundle of blankets and pillows (WILLY).

Counterpane (MARTHA).

4 small black notebooks (MARY).

2 wicker chairs (MELLING).

Stethoscope (JEFFREYS).

Red tray.   *On it :* 3 cups of hot coffee (JOSEPHINE).

2 bundles of newspapers (JOSEPHINE).

Personal.

JEFFREYS : fountain pen, cigarette case with cigarettes, matches.

SCENE 2

Strike.

Newspapers from floor.

Cup and saucer from desk.

Tidy desk.   Replace box of sweets on bookcase.

Set.

Embroidery frame L.C.   *On it :* tapestry without hole.

Stool above frame.

Stool of embroidery frame. *Set on stool :* tray of paints, rag, palette, paint brushes in jam jar, pencils.

On chair L. of desk : toolbag, hammer.

On L. end of desk : newspaper cuttings in bulldog clip.

On stool up L. : SARAT'S coat.

Fire on.

Electric fittings on.

Off Stage. Bucket of logs (MARTHA).

Personal. MELLING : clasp knife, wrist-watch.

ACT III
SCENE 1

Set.

On desk : embroidery books, sheet of drawing paper, jam jar of clean water with two paint brushes in it, rag.

Replace bulldog clip in desk drawer.

On window seat : newspapers.

Move chair from L. of stove to L. of desk.

Stove on.

Electric fittings off.

Off stage.

Bag. *In it :* stethoscope, bottles, etc., surgical gauze with cutting folded inside (JEFFREYS).

Embroidery book (MARY).

Sewing (MARY).

SCENE 2

Setting as Act I.

Set.

On chair above table : MELLING'S jacket.

On table : ashtray.

L. *of staircase :* 3 suitcases, roll of bedding.

Stool from down R. to R. of the armchair L.C.

Electric fittings on.

Fire on.

Off Stage.

Book, sewing, workbasket (MARY).

Basket of food (JOSEPHINE).

Bunch of snowdrops (WILLY).

Bag. *In it :* gauze and cutting, roll of surgical tape, roll of red tape, scissors (JEFFREYS).

Overcoat (JEFFREYS).

Personal.

JEFFREYS : cigarette case with cigarettes, matches.

MARY : newspaper cutting.

LIGHTING PLOT

ACT I

To open.

All lights checked to ½.
Fittings switched off.
Fire on.
Daylight through stained-glass window.

Cue 1.—At rise of Curtain, commence slow dim to out of daylight through the window.

Cue 2.—JOSEPHINE switches on lights. All lights full up, fittings on.

ACT II

SCENE 1

To open.

All lights checked to ½.
Fittings switched on.
Stove on.
Twilight outside window.

No cues.

SCENE 2

To open.

All lights checked to ½.
Fittings switched on.
Stove on.
Twilight outside window.

Cue 1.—When the MOTHER SUPERIOR burns the cuttings, bring up stove and flicker.

ACT III

SCENE 1

To open.

All lights full up.
Fittings switched off.
Stove on.
Daylight outside window.

No cues.

SCENE 2

To open.

All lights full up.
Fittings switched on.
Fire on.
Daylight through windows.

No cues.